HOLY
Ground
A Faith Story

6/10/04
Dear Karen —
All God's blessings!
Carolyn Hughes

Carolyn Hughes

Published by:
Loaves and Fishes Press, PO Box 268, Kendall Park, NJ 08824

In accord with Canon 827 of the New Code of Canon Law, this publication has been submitted to a censor of the Diocese and nothing being found contrary to faith and morals, we hereby grant permission in accord with Canon 824 that it be published.
        Rev. Msgr. John B. Szymanski, Vicar General, Diocese of Metuchen
        sAugust 8, 2000

N.B. The ecclesiatical permission implies nothing more than the material contained in the publication has been examined by diocesan censors and nothing contrary to faith and morals has been found therein.
        Rev. David I. Fulton, Censor of Books
        Diocese of Metuchen

ISBN: 0-9744469-0-4   LCCCN: 2003096652

The publisher gratefully acknowledges the use of the following materials:
    Church Documents Reference Suite (Boston: Pauline Software, Pauline Books & Media, 8th edition); *Favorite Novenas and Prayers*, Norma Cronin Cassidy, editor (New York: Paulist Press, 1972); *In Search of the Sacred: Contributions to an Answer*, Josef Pieper (San Francisco: Ignatius Press, 1991); *A Priest Forever: The Life of Father Eugene Hamilton,* Father Benedict J. Groeschel, C.F.R. (Huntington, IN: Our Sunday Visitor Publishing Division, 1998).

The following excerpted works are used with permission of the publisher:
    From *The Collected Works of St. John of the Cross*, translated by Kieran Kavanaugh and Otilio Rodriguez Copyright © 1964, 1979, 1991 by Washington Province of Discalced Carmelites. ICS Publications, 2131 Lincoln Road, N.E., Washington, DC 20002-1199 U.S.A. www.icspublications.org.

    From *The Collected Works of St. Teresa of Avila, Volume One*, translated by Kieran Kavanaugh and Otilio Rodriguez Copyright © 1976 by Washington Province of Discalced Carmelites. ICS Publications, 2131 Lincoln Road, N.E., Washington, DC 20002-1199 U.S.A. www.icspublications.org.

    Excerpts from the *New American Bible* with Revised New Testament and Psalms Copyright © 1986, 1970 Confraternity of Christian Doctrine, Inc., Washington, DC. Used with permission. All rights reserved. No portion of the *New American Bible* may be reprinted without permission in writing from the copyright holder.

    English translation of the *Catechism of the Catholic Church* for the United States of America copyright © 1994, United States Catholic Conference, Inc. – Libreria Editrice Vaticana. English translation of the: *Catechism of the Cahtolic Church Modifications from the Editio Typica* copyright © 1997, United States Catholic Conference, Inc. – Liberia Editrice Vaticana. Used with permission.

    Excerpts from the English translation of *The General Instruction of the Roman Missal* © 2002, International Committee on English in the Liturgy, Inc. All rights reserved.

Carolyn Hughes' life in and with the Holy Spirit is an exciting story of a valiant woman of the modern Church who is a wife, mother and committed parishioner, as well as a journalist of note. She remains true to her spiritual roots, but wonderfully open to the "still, small voice of God" speaking to her from her earliest years until the present time.

St. Augustine was converted when he heard a child's voice telling him "Tolle Lege - take and read." You will be blessed abundantly if you take and read this book with half the ardor of that great saint.

Father Gerald P. Ruane
Sacred Heart Institute of Healing

This book is a reflection of the incredible love that Carolyn Hughes has for her God, and for her brothers and sisters who make up his family. She has taken faith sharing to new heights by revealing to us, as the true journalist she is, the way that human lives are touched by the divine and forever changed. And we are all the richer for her having shared her story.

Rayanne Damiano
'The Catholic Spirit,' Diocese of Metuchen

Acknowledgements

Without my husband Steve by my side, you would not be reading this book. I sincerely thank him for his love, patience and valuable suggestions as this book took shape in many wee hours of the morning.

I also thank those who encouraged me on the way to publication, especially Most. Rev. Edward T. Hughes, Bishop Emeritus of Metuchen; Msgr. Donald M. Endebrock; Father Benedict J. Groeschel, C.F.R.; Father Gerald P. Ruane; Father Robert G. Lynam; Father Sylvester Catallo, O.F.M. Cap.; Florence and Ed Belding, Julie Ferrara, and Rayanne Damiano, all of whom read and critiqued the draft, as well as the members of my parish prayer group, "Children of the Light," St. Augustine of Canterbury, Kendall Park, N.J., for their prayer support.

A special thanks goes to Clara Baumann for her layout and graphic design, and to Karen Wasliewski, for her assistance with cover design ideas in the early stages of this book's life.

In loving memory of my late parents,
Helen and Stanley,
in gratitude for the gift of life
and of my Catholic faith.

Table of Contents

Table of Contents (cont.)

Foreword

All of us who believe walk on holy ground. All of us who believe encounter God in varied ways on our journey of faith. But many of us do not reflect deeply on the holy ground we walk upon. Many of us do not reflect prayerfully enough on the truth that we encounter God constantly on our faith journey. Carolyn Hughes has reflected prayerfully on the holy ground she treads and upon the God she meets at every turn of the road. In this book she tells her faith story to all who will listen. And she does so because, like every Catholic, she is called to bear witness to the faith that guides her life – a faith deeply rooted in the Eucharist.

This is a very personal story of God's presence in her life. It takes courage to share such intimate faith experiences, especially in a world that seems to doubt the very possibility of a personal relationship with God. But Carolyn does not hesitate, beginning with the powerful awareness of Jesus' love flowing to her from the tabernacle at a time when she was only three years old. Many of her experiences of God's loving, caring, healing presence may seem unusual and startling. We're tempted to say that such experiences are so foreign to us that we cannot relate to her story. But her true message is that all of us have our own encounters with God. We just have to recognize them, reflect on them and see them as God's special, graced gifts to us. God meets each one of us in His own unique manner and at His own special times. It is good to share these blessed moments with others. Indeed, such sharing leads us to a deeper awareness that God is always with us, drawing us closer together as His family, the Church.

Carolyn writes as a wife and mother, as a member of the Catholic Church with a deep appreciation for its tradition and its teaching. Often those who share their personal stories fail to develop a sound doctrinal foundation. Not so here. She writes within the framework of authentic Catholic theology. Her sources are the Scriptures, the teachings of the Church, the Papal documents, the classic, mystical writers, such as St. John of the Cross and St. Teresa of Avila, and sound modern theologians. Her special talent is to root her personal experiences in the wider life of the Church. Her call to closeness to her Lord is bound up with the Sacraments; with the universal call to holiness through Baptism; with the gifts of the Holy Spirit through Confirmation; and especially with the Eucharist which is the thread that ties the whole book together. So too, she sees Mary as constantly calling her children to gather around Jesus, especially in the Eucharist.

This book is realistic in its recognition of evil in the world and the ceaseless attacks of the evil one himself, but always with the deepest conviction that God's power can overcome all evil. Carolyn's own life has not been easy. Sickness and suffering, the battle against cancer and the resulting financial problems have plagued her and her family. She shares her sense of desolation at the feeling of God's absence during her own dark night. But she testifies also to the healing, saving power of suffering united to that of Jesus – the power of the cross to save if only we embrace it. Running through all the suffering is the divine invitation to the deep joy and peace that flow from faith in God's love for us.

Carolyn's final chapter is a moving testimony to the goodness of the Lord – a goodness that brings her and all of us to that deep inner silence where He alone speaks to our hearts. It is also a call to the cross and to that holiness which consists in doing the Father's Will wherever that may lead us. This final chapter is the author's personal profession of faith. It is faith in a loving, forgiving Father, revealed to us in Jesus through the power of the Holy Spirit. It is faith in Mary, our Mother; in the Church, its teaching and its Sacraments. It is faith in the power of prayer and in the call to share God's love with all our brothers and sisters.

In this final chapter, one sentence gives the reason for the book's existence. Carolyn writes: "We share our own joy, our own story, so that others might know how loved, unique and, by God's choice, necessary we all are to the Father who created us." May we all experience the deep peace that comes from sharing God's love. This is a book that deserves our prayerful reflection.

+Edward T. Hughes
Bishop Emeritus of Metuchen
March, 2003

Introduction

The world as we know it changed Sept. 11, 2001. The horror of the terrorist attacks by Islamic militants using commercial aircraft as weapons dispelled any doubts of the terrible reality of hatred, sin and death in our world today. The ways that we think, feel and live have changed.

About 3,000 innocent people died that day as they went about their daily lives in New York, Washington and Pennsylvania. Husbands, wives, fathers, mothers, grandmothers and grandfathers were gone in a violent jolt that snuffed out their lives with shocking and evil brutality. The rituals of religious faith suddenly became something in which most people found solace and comfort. Some dubbed it a "wake-up call."

On a certain level, I believe that because of Sept. 11, we all experienced that there is more than this passing world. Somehow, I truly believe that *if we are honest with ourselves*, we all knew, even for a brief moment, that there is more. Looking at the many young widows with little ones in tow, we knew that there *has* to be more. It was clear at least on some level that spending our life on ambition, the false treasures of earthly trinkets and power, is a waste of time. Faith matters. Love alone matters, and love is eternal.

This is not a new message to Christianity. This *is* the message of Christianity. For us, God is Love, and as Catholic

Christians, we believe that He sent His only Son, Jesus, to die and rise from the dead to save humanity from its sins — its many, brutal, horrifying sins. Faith in Jesus isn't something to be put aside, explained away by inadequate scientific theories, and taken out only when it is deemed to be needed. Faith is for all times, all places, all situations, and all people. And it is meant to be shared.

That's how this book began. It was a collection of memories that I wrote down as a gift to my mother, the late Helen Mikutel, to share how present God had been in my life, to help her prepare for her own death from ovarian cancer. These were things that my mom never knew about my life, and I wanted her to know before she died. These memories somehow became organized and grew into a book to be shared beyond my family, at the suggestion of friends and co-workers along the way. It was completed before Sept. 11.

The events of last year only confirmed more powerfully for me that the Christian faith is meant for every day of one's life. That is at the heart of this book's message. Living a life of Christian faith in love with God, loving and serving His people for love of Him – living the Eucharist – is the only way to true peace and justice in the world. It isn't outdated, nor unhealthy as some might say, or stupid, or elitist. It is the Truth.

While our modern world has made much progress in some areas, it has welcomed evil with open arms on many levels. Everything has turned inside out. Choosing evil has become "good"; choosing the good has become "evil", and often illegal. We have not solved humanity's problems; we have only suc-ceeded in creating more and worse problems. And we are too proud to admit it, or too dependent on blood money depen-dent on an industry that lives on the death of others, such as abortion and embryonic stem cell research.

Our modern world has been looking for Love in all the wrong places.

It's time to look again at the Catholic faith, the "Mother Church" of Christianity. "The world" equates love only with sex and pleasure. Yet even the pagan Greek philosophers were not as ignorant on the whole as our world is today. They understood that levels of love exist. We seemingly don't. School teachers and Planned Parenthood school-based clinics can send our underage daughters for abortions without our knowledge or consent. This is love?

It's time to commit, or recommit, to the journey of faith,

hope and love that alone offers the fullest answer to the "incurable wound" of evil in our world. We are being given a special opportunity to face the Truth: Jesus is present in His Catholic Church in the fullest sense in this world, especially in the Sacrament of the Eucharist. He alone can save us from ourselves. He alone can promise the joy of forgiveness and peace, not only in this life, but also in the next. He alone has conquered sin and the power of death. And it is He who established the Church.

The Roman Catholic Church has stood its ground, on "holy ground" with constant hope, through more than 2,000 years — through scandals, divisions and countless empty philosophies and evil regimes. And because of Jesus' Presence in the Church through the power of the Holy Spirit we will continue to stand our ground, moving out against the "gates of hell" that cannot prevail against us, even when evil infiltrates the Church itself. For as the Second Vatican Council so beautifully taught, the Church is much more than its very necessary hierarchy. All of its members are the Church as well. We – the clergy, religious and, by far largest in numbers, the laity — are truly the Church, together!

Please try to see the Catholic faith and the incredible Love of Jesus in this book through my experience of the "holy ground" of a very ordinary life spent in the light of God's Love in simple ways. And please don't let the "wake-up call" of 9/11 leave you empty. Fill your heart with Jesus. Come to the Eucharist. Come to Life.

CHAPTER 1

Holiness: It's Our Call

May the heart of Jesus in the most Blessed Sacrament
be praised, adored and loved,
with grateful affection,
at every moment,
in all the tabernacles of the world,
even until the end of time. Amen.
Traditional prayer

My first memory of meeting the Lord Jesus is a very beautiful one. It is one of the most precious memories of my life. I share it because through this experience God my Father taught me some very important things about the Real Presence of Jesus in the celebration of the Eucharist and in the Blessed Sacrament. I also share it because this encounter became the foundation of my entire life, and Jesus, our Eucharistic Lord, became its center.

I was just a baby, about three years old. My younger sister Nancy had not yet been born because I remember that I still slept in the crib, and when she arrived I was moved into a "big bed." My sister Barbara came along five years after I was born. I knew at that tender age what love was. I knew the love of my parents and family for me, and was familiar with how it felt to be loved — safe and secure. I was soon to learn more about God's love in a very unexpected way.

I think that my parents had taken me to church a few times. I was so young that the votive candles flickering in the fragile metal candlestands in the front of the church frightened me. My child's mind could imagine them tipping over and starting a fire.

The sanctuary and altar of Our Lady of Consolation Church in Brooklyn, my childhood parish, is ornate and glittering, very appealing to the curious eyes of a little child. I was especially fascinated by the beautiful gold "box" in the center of the altar. I do not recall having ever been told anything about what it was. But surrounded by many brightly-lit candles and candelabras, it was fascinating to me on that particular day when my parents brought me to church, probably for a wedding of some of their friends. Little did I know that I, too, would fall in love — forever.

My eyes were again drawn to the gold "box" in the center of the altar. In fact, I remember not being able to take my eyes off of it. I believe that the wedding ceremony had not yet begun, for there was no one in the sanctuary. All at once and without words, I became powerfully aware of a love that embraced me directly from the "box" on the altar. This love was silent and gentle, yet it was as if a fiery dart had left the altar with tremendous speed and power, piercing my heart, for that was where I experienced this Presence. I knew that there was a real Person gazing at me from that beautiful "box" and I was overwhelmed with love like I had never known.

At that moment, it did not matter that it was impossible for someone to fit inside a little gold box. I knew, even as so young a child, that this was not a concern, and that was grace. As I look back at this life-changing moment, it was as if I was being hugged all over, from the inside out. I experienced a burning in my heart, a warmth that radiated through every part of me. All at once, I experienced that I was loved and safe — beautiful and wanted — very tiny and helpless, yet protected and filled with joy — a joy that has never left me.

I could never again doubt that there was Someone in the world who loved me with an unbelievable love. And being just a baby I did what came naturally; I loved Him back. I remember wanting to cuddle up to Him. It was the most natural thing in the world to do in response to His touch. I did not even have a name for Him yet but I loved Him. I had a hard time leaving the church that day, because I had never been happier than when that wonderful Presence wrapped me up in unseen arms.

———————

It seems to me that many of us go through life at light speed, never noticing the graced encounters our loving God arranges all around us every single day.

The Lord has not allowed me to do that; He has gifted me in countless ways with marvelous touches of divine Love, as in the experience I just shared. He has sheltered me always in His Eucharistic Presence. He has gradually taught me with great patience since early childhood how to see Him in the smallest and most ordinary things and places. And I believe that He would like me to share some of these "life lessons" with you.

I feel that way because stories of faith are powerful and can have profound effects on people's lives. That belief was con-firmed during my five-year ministry as a staff writer for ***The Catholic Spirit*** newspaper, Diocese of Metuchen, New Jersey, where I now am a correspondent. I'm constantly moved by stories of faith, courage and hope I am privileged to hear in my everyday work. Every one of us has a unique and beautiful faith story to tell, because every one of us *is* a unique and beautiful story written by the hand of God.

In my faith journey, the Lord has taken me through deep valleys, even through the valley of the shadow of death, and lifted me up to the heights where I have known His gentle love in wonderful ways. Sometimes these have been in ways that for the most part are expected in cloisters or monasteries, more often to those who have "left the world" and not to those like myself with busy, full lives of raising children and balancing the budget, right in the middle of "the world."

God has surprised me in His self-revelations and taught me much about Himself over the years. Above all, I wish to give God the glory for being so holy and generous, and this book is first of all a "thank you" to Him. But I also believe that together, you and I can draw nearer to the Lord through the reflections that follow.

My prayer for you is that you will find yourself in these pages. My hope is that you will find hope in its consolations and courage in its trials for your own life's journey. I firmly believe with St. Paul that as Christians we live for one another when we live for the Lord Jesus. Therefore, each of our lives is meant to touch and console the lives of others, through prayer support, redemptive suffering, and consolation and comfort, as St. Paul so beautifully states in his second letter to the

Corinthians. This book is very much based upon his insights in
2 Cor. 1: 3-7:

> Blessed be the God and Father of our Lord Jesus Christ,
> the Father of compassion and God of all encouragement,
> who encourages us in our every affliction, so that we
> may be able to encourage those who are in any affliction
> with the encouragement with which we ourselves are
> encouraged by God. For as Christ's sufferings overflow
> to us, so through Christ does our encouragement also
> overflow. If we are afflicted, it is for your encouragement
> and salvaiton; if we are encouraged, it is for your
> encouragement, which enables you to endure the same
> sufferings that we suffer. Our hope for you is firm, for
> we know that as you share in the sufferings, you also
> share in the encouragement . . .

I hope that you will discover a very loving, approachable
God Who is incomparably accessible yet always beyond our
understanding, and Who takes us far more seriously than any
of us take ourselves. Above all, I pray that you discover and
accept His Love in a deeper and a new way, for the Lord
approaches each of us in a manner that is perfect for every
individual. God mysteriously calls us to travel by different
roads, but He graces us to deal with whatever circumstances
our own individual journey brings. The key is always His will,
His grace and our "yes".

This is not a "how-to" book of instructions on our faith
journey or a doctrinal dissertation. I do hope it encourages you
to examine your own faith story, see how God is working in
your life and be motivated to learn more about your faith as

well. It is for each of us to decide to make faith in Jesus our number one priority instead of other things like work or pleasures, although each of those has its place. I pray that you will decide to embrace the Kingdom of God as your own in a new and deeper way, and then see where your own story goes.

I know that there are risks in sharing personal details of one's spiritual life and I do not approach this task lightly. Sometimes God has touched me in what some might call "extraordinary" ways. I believe that God *is* extraordinary — that life itself is extraordinary — and that every touch of God is a *sign* to all of us who need reassurance on what can be very difficult faith walks. Perhaps we limit the Lord by assigning certain graces as extraordinary. Perhaps we need to re-examine our definitions and expectations.

I say that because I have come to see that God still sends His tokens of love however He chooses — to children and mothers and fathers, as well as to priests and religious, as Vatican Council II emphasized in its recognition of the universal call to holiness for all of God's people (**Lumen Gentium, Chapter V**). The Lord works in profound ways in people with very ordinary lives like myself, and I believe that He always has. I have come to understand His surprising graces as "lights" in the darkness in a Godless age, calling us back to the Lord. They have been lights for me and I pray that they will be lights for you as well, inspiring you to step out in faith and take the risk of letting the Lord into your life more deeply.

I have often thought over the years that there are lessons

and insights to be shared in my faith journey, because I have seen them so clearly as lessons for myself. But that alone did not convince me that this book should be written. Because it is so personal, I set it in the back of my mind for years, waiting patiently for the Lord to make it clear to me if I should write. And the years moved on as I occasionally sensed that, yes, this book should be, but it just did not seem to be the right time.

I was finally "surprised" by the Holy Spirit into the realization that it was, indeed, time to begin writing. It was while driving home from Pennsylvania through the Delaware Water Gap on U.S. Route 80 east in New Jersey one very ordinary day that the Lord sent what was for me a startling "sign", finally convincing me that the time had come to begin writing.

My husband Steve and I owned a second home hidden away in the woods in the Pocono Mountains of Pennsylvania for more than a decade. The number of times we have driven to and from the mountains through the Delaware Water Gap, which spans both our home state of New Jersey and Pennsylvania, are countless.

I had been thinking about writing this book at the time. As I maneuvered through the winding portion of Route 80, my attention was caught by something unusual on the side of the road. The road was in the process of being resurfaced and the portion I was driving through at that time had a large mass of asphalt piled up off the lanes to the right. It was intensely black, so dark that the figure I saw walking in front of it was all the more sharply contrasted against this coal-black background.

It was a beautiful white dove.

I literally gasped as I drove past, looking again for the few seconds I was given, at a dove simply walking next to the highway, seemingly unaffected by the traffic racing by. My heart knew at that moment that it was a sign for me, since this was not the first time that a dove had literally walked into my life just at the right moment. After reading the chapter entitled "Holy Spirit" you'll understand better its personal significance.

Also, when my mother Helen Mikutel was diagnosed with ovarian cancer, the Lord graciously gave her four years with us until He took her home in January 2000. I wanted to share some of my deepest experiences of the Lord with her before she died so that she might know and love Him more, and came to see that,s at least partly, Jesus gave me this time to say my own "goodbye" and "thank you" through these pages. This desire was my most powerful incentive to write as I raced the clock and succeeded; she did read it and the Lord blessed us both through it.

And so began the long process of doing the actual work, squeezing time in between a family, a very demanding full-time writing job and ministries within the Church. At first, I kept waiting for that ideal time when I would be able to sit down and accomplish something in long stretches. I ended up simply waiting and getting nothing done. It was when I finally realized that I had to stay up that "extra" hour past midnight or snatch a brief half an hour between other activities, with no opportunities to write for long periods of time, that I got rolling.

Gradually, the pieces fell together as I organized the chapters, which are only partially chronological. Because I believe that real life is a blend of profound and everyday experiences, and that the "ordinary" experiences of life are as charged with the glory of God as are the dramatic ones we tend to recall more easily, I have deliberately let the chapters flow much like life flows. The days and years between the major moments of our lives are not just fillers; they are always exciting because the Lord is to be found in every moment of our lives. In fact, the present moment is the only place we truly can find the Lord. That is partially the power of prayer — its ability to pull us out of our preoccupation with the past and the future, and keep us squarely in the only little piece of time we are ever given, the present moment, where we meet the God whose name is "I AM." The moments of spiritual import in our lives are built on our faithfulness to the Lord in the ordinary, sometimes dull, sometimes painful, moments; as the Gospels tell us, to be trusted in greater things we must be trustworthy in the little things first.

Sometimes I have also experienced God's Presence directly and powerfully in what might be called "mystical" encounters. Every religion has a mystical aspect, but Christian mystical theology differs from that of other religions in several significant ways. It is both Trinitarian and Incarnational — that is, it is through Jesus Christ, who is both God and man, that the Christian relates to God, who is Father, Son and Holy Spirit. Catholic mysticism expresses the fullness of the Christian mystical experience in that it is also Eucharistic, reflecting the fullness of Christ's teaching about His Real Presence in the

Sacrament of the Eucharist. It follows then that the Catholic mystical tradition cannot be understood apart from Scripture and Church teaching, while not adding anything substantial to public revelation.

In this book, I will speak about only Christian mysticism, and specifically Catholic mystical encounters because this is my faith tradition. Mystical experience can be described as a direct experience and knowledge of God in Love — as an encounter of God as He is in Himself beyond images and symbols. It is a free gift of grace. It can be said that those who experience God in such a way are not content just to know about Him; they long for union with Him through contemplation, a gift of prayer that grows as the soul draws closer to its divine Lord.

Most modern Catholics have heard of Saint Francis of Assisi, and perhaps the 16th century Carmelite Saints John of the Cross and Teresa of Avila, or Saint Catherine of Siena, for example. Some might even know that they were all teachers of the Catholic mystical tradition in their own times who continue to influence our own day. What most people may not realize is that the Catholic, and thus the Christian, mystical tradition has very deep roots.

Loosely examined, the Christian mystical tradition extends back to the Church Fathers of the early centuries, who transformed the language and thought of the Greek philosophers and specifically of Plato's idea of the soul's relationship to God, in their mystical theology. The monastic tradition and especially the thought of St. Augustine of Hippo influenced the

Latin West and the mystical theology of the Middle Ages.
Differences in mystical theology developed over the centuries. A
separate tradition developed in the Eastern Church as well. In
**The Origins of the Christian Mystical Tradition: From
Plato to Denys**, author Andrew Louth notes that the Fathers'
writings are more theoretical, in contrast to the more affective
writings found in later Western mysticism, but that there is still a
common thread that unites them. That thread is the longing of
the soul for union with God in Christ. Union with Christ is also
union with His Body, the Church, especially gathered at Eucharist. True Christian, true Catholic mysticism is never a solitary
thing, like that of some non-Christian religions.

For the saints, for all serious Christians and for some others
of different faiths who have pursued the truth sincerely outside
Christianity in good conscience, the goal of the journey has not
changed. It is union with God on earth and eternally in
heaven. As followers of Christ, we believe that we are made
in the image and likeness of God, and that union with God
is what we are all made for. Over the past few centuries,
some spiritual writers have taken the position that the grace
of contemplative prayer — very simply described as a
simple, loving gaze at the Lord that is beyond words and
images — is a universal call for every Christian. Others have
stated that it is a special call given only to some. It seems
possible to me from my own limited experience that there is
truth in both positions, especially in light of the Second
Vatican Council's universal call to holiness. I believe that all
Christians are called to some degree of contemplation; I

believe that there is a mystical dimension to *every* encounter with the Lord, simply because we encounter a God who is ultimately mystery, and mystery is never ordinary. Therefore, it seems to me that the degree of contemplation to which one is called is determined by the Lord and one's cooperation with His Will, for God alone is aware of His perfect plan and how each of us fits into that plan.

Several mystical and spiritual writers have left us what can be thought of almost as a "map" of the spiritual journey, sometimes referred to as the traditional Christian "three ways" of the spiritual life. These three ways or stages are called the purgative, illuminative and unitive stages. Very simply stated, they describe those beginning the journey, those growing in the life of the Lord and those who have reached spiritual maturity.

Franciscan Friar of the Renewal Father Benedict J. Groeschel develops these stages and relates them to modern life in his book ***Spiritual Passages: The Psychology of Spiritual Development***. In it he notes that we are, in a certain sense, at all stages at any given time, but predominantly at only one point (pg. 119). What is important is that the God who ordered the universe calls His children in an orderly way, and that He calls each and every one of us because of His love for us.

St. John of the Cross wrote primarily for fellow priests and religious sisters about 400 years ago in Spain, and until Vatican Council II, it was expected for the most part that only those chosen by God to serve in Church vocations would be serious enough about their faith to benefit from his wisdom. But I agree with the authors of the Council documents that nothing can be further from the truth. We are all called through Baptism to be serious about our faith. Therefore, the roadmap provided by the great Christian mystical writers can still be followed and adapted to our particular situations.

Union with God, a state of indescribable peace and habitual sense of the Lord's Presence — of profound inner transformation and contemplation of God even in the midst of great activity — is usually preceded by trials and difficulties that are meant to purify the soul. St. John of the Cross, in particular, explained the dynamics of these purifying trials when it seems as if God has abandoned the soul. He named the most intense periods of purification the Dark Night of the Senses and the Dark Night of the Soul.

I have learned over the years that we all go through our own "dark nights" or "darknesses". They are very real and are used by God as a means of growth, although they are most often not St. John's most intense purification of the Dark Night of the Soul. Sometimes we cause our own darknesses by our disobedience or refusal to give up sinful habits. There are no short cuts on the spiritual journey and many lesser episodes of darkness generally precede the profound interior darkness of the Dark Night, but they are not of lesser importance. All times of darkness can draw us nearer to Our Lord and that is a great blessing.

It is my hope that my own experience in the chapter

entitled "Lessons in the Darkness" can help you to recognize
that the hand of God is very present in the darkest times of
your own life, and encourage you not to give up when things
get difficult no matter what, _because the prize of drawing closer to the
Lord is worth any price._ How the Lord worked with me is not
presented as a norm. My experience seems to combine ele-
ments of several spiritual writers, because God works differently with every person.

I realize that some readers might still question how several
of the ways that God has touched my life could be relevant for
them. Some might dismiss them as being "nice" for me but
not the way that God works in their own life. Others might
think them too "different". I have therefore tried to include
connections to the life of the Christian today in the modern
world, especially at the suggestion of the Most Rev. Edward T.
Hughes, bishop emeritus of the Diocese of Metuchen. I
include many references to papal documents, especially those
of Pope John Paul II; the documents of Vatican Council II; the
new **Catechism of the Catholic Church**, and the writings of
the saints. I am especially grateful to Bishop Hughes and my
spiritual director of many years, Msgr. Donald M. Endebrock,
former chairman of the theological commission of the
Metuchen Diocese, for having been my mentors in this effort.

In addition, and very importantly, I believe that one need
not experience everything another person has experienced in
order to benefit from it; there is always some inner message at
the heart of any experience that is applicable to all. In **_Spiri-_**

tual Passages (*pgs. 6-11*), Father Groeschel draws from classical, spiritual and psychological sources and gives an insightful description, I believe, of what he calls the "four voices of God." These "voices" describe in general how unique individuals respond to the divine call to deeper intimacy — to God as One, True, Good or Beautiful. Father Groeschel believes that all people fit into at least one and possibly two categories, and that the categories are not exact but they are comprehensive.

Those who seek God as One are people who live in pursuit of intellectual and emotional " integration" of internal and contradictory forces within themselves. Such spiritual seekers will find peace in striving for God as unity in chaos. In fact, such a person will not find true peace except in the unity offered in God, Father Groeschel states.

Intellectual pursuit of God as Truth is similar to responding to God as One, but the individuals who seek God as Truth are calmer and experience less inner turmoil, Father Groeschel continues. He cites St. Thomas Aquinas as a classic example of one who sought God as Truth, and found it in a profound personal revelation late in life. The danger for these people is that they can waste too much time thinking and forget about seeking, being distracted by the very intellectual pursuits that were originally intended to bring one nearer to God, the ultimate Truth.

Father Groeschel describes the two other types as also being similar to one another — those who seek God as Good or as Beautiful. Those who are drawn to God as Good are depicted as affectionate and warm people who, if they remain faithful to God's call to a deeper spiritual life, become spontaneously involved in generous charitable works. St. Francis of Assisi is the classic example given here.

This type of seeker is usually very sensitive and can become easily disillusioned. Straying from the pursuit of the only Source of infinite goodness can be disastrous for such a person, Father Groeschel explains.

Finally, there are those who seek God as Beauty, as did St. Augustine of Hippo. This type of person can easily be caught up in the pleasure of encountering beauty and thus be sidetracked in reaching the ultimate Source of all true Beauty. Father Groeschel advises those who experience God as Beauty that repentance is essential, since such a person will tend to fall and rise again.

Once more, as is the case in every category, the danger is always settling for less than God. Once more, the Lord calls His people in an orderly fashion. I therefore ask that you pray that the Holy Spirit reveals a special message that is meant for you as you read these pages. He alone can inspire you with the next step you need to take in your spiritual journey, but it does help to have some idea of how one responds to the inner call of God. Self-knowledge is a necessity for spiritual growth.

I expect that some might think that my obvious belief in satan is "outdated" at best or "crazy" at worst, or that the Church and the world are too sophisticated to truly believe that the Lord can still work miracles. Scripture and Church teaching have always upheld the truth of personal evil spirits, and miracles are standard fare in the canonization process for a saint.

Although several of my experiences may be called extraordinary, I do not define them as "miracles" in the textbook sense of the word for reasons that vary in every case. But they meant a great deal to me, and I'm convinced that several chapters truly document events that seem to operate outside natural laws, most notably in the many ways that God has healed me.

I entrust this work in a special way to the Holy Spirit, the Spirit of love and life. I have a deep love for Him, and have come to count on His inspiration and gifts of grace with confidence in His love for me.

Every experience of God's Love has made me aware of His infinite Love for each one of us. We are children of the same Father in heaven and Jesus' Holy Spirit intimately connects us all, especially in Eucharist. Therefore, know that a prayer for you is attached to these pages, in His Love.

May the Lord Jesus bless you and fill your heart with His peace.

CHAPTER 2

Jesus, Children and Prayer

Psalm 8

O LORD, our Lord,

how awesome is your name through all the earth!

You have set your majesty above the heavens!

Out of the mouths of babes and infants

you have drawn a defense against your foes,

to silence enemy and avenger. *(2-3)*

I do not know exactly when I was able to connect Jesus in the Blessed Sacrament with the Person who had reached out from the tabernacle and touched my heart that day as a young child. But I believe that shortly thereafter, possibly from my grandmother, I learned that it was the Lord Jesus in the "box" called the tabernacle.

Every day waiting for my First Communion seemed endless, and I have not yet found words to describe that union of Jesus' Heart with mine for the first time. I couldn't help but think about Jesus a great deal and couldn't wait to receive Him at Mass and be near Him in the Blessed Sacrament. Every time I was in the Lord's Presence that same glorious warmth and Love enveloped me, although not always in the same extraordinary way. I realize now that one touch by the Lord was enough to cause me to love Him for a lifetime.

From the moment I experienced the love of Jesus from the tabernacle, just thinking about Him caused me to relive some of that same captivating love. In time, I recognized that those thoughts and the loving exchange between a little girl and the Lord were really prayer. They were simple, affectionate childlike responses to the God who loved me, since I was, after all, just a child.

In retrospect, my own experience of Jesus in the tabernacle taught me about the prayers of children and how we, too, must always become as little children if we wish to hear the Lord's voice speaking to us, if we wish to be open to His Presence in our lives. Many people today seem to believe that the prayers of children are powerful, but that is about as far as most people seem to think the spiritual life of a child can go. A developmental approach to the spiritual life has become popular and it has some merit, but like any human understanding, it has limitations. Developmental theories based exclusively on psychological observations may not leave room for the work of grace. But the great spiritual masters, the mystics and the great saints, always wisely allowed room for God's almighty hand.

In her book ***Interior Castle***, St. Teresa of Avila beautifully illustrates the power of God's grace using an analogy of water. At first, the pilgrim must do much work to collect the "water" of grace, as water must be drawn out of a deep well bucket by bucket. Prayer is truly work for the beginner in the spiritual life. As the pilgrim remains faithful, it becomes easier to draw water because someone is helping. In the case of prayer, that someone is God Himself. Finally, prayer is no longer work for the spiritually mature. God Himself pours the water of grace into the soul just as an irrigation system delivers water to the parched fields. Ultimately, Teresa is emphasizing that it is always God Who is the source of all grace.

It seems to me from my own experience that if we apply developmental rules too rigidly we run the risk of presuming that children cannot experience God in any significant way. Or we might assume that spiritual growth is somehow entirely age-related and something we can therefore easily predict and control. Some believe that children are incapable of understanding the mystery of Christ because they are too young, but the fact is that we are all incapable of understanding the mystery of Christ at *any* age. *Everything is grace.* Children teach us a great deal just by being children, especially that to enter the Kingdom of God we must become children at heart. We have to trust Jesus completely and take Him at His word.

The bottom line is that it is always God who loves us first (***John 3:16***.) It is He, a God of surprises, who lets Himself be known (***John 14:21***). The Spirit alone penetrates and reveals the depths of God (***Acts 2:10***). We can never take credit for His revelation and my own experience confirms that. It always is the work of grace, no matter how old we are (or aren't) or how many years we have loved and served God. It has never been, nor will it ever be, anything or anyway else.

In retrospect, I realize that the Lord's touch gave my life direction and purpose before I could even put words to those concepts. Jesus became my life when I was just a tiny child because that is when He chose to introduce Himself. It did not matter how young I was; what I was lacking He supplied in grace, just as He continues to do today, as my husband Steve and I enjoy two lovely young granddaughters, Kayla and Brittany.

Over the years I have seen again and again that God's touch is different in each of our lives but that it is *always* there, unique and perfect for our own individual needs, perfectly timed by a perfect Creator. Without claiming to be an expert on children's spirituality, I have come to see that some of the most beautiful spiritual songs are sung in the lives of the littlest members of the human family who are not even able to communicate them to the adult world. In their innocence and simple faith — in their inability to take personal credit for what only God can do — the youngest of hearts are especially open to the Lord's revelation of His deepest secrets (**Luke 10:21-22**). Children show us the way to the heart of the Lord.

All that had been necessary for the Lord to touch me was that my parents bring me to the right place at the right time. God did the rest. It is up to us to bring ourselves and our children to Him, for they are really *His* children, where He can be found — in His Church (**Matt. 19:14**). The greatest gift we can offer to the next generations is our faith. For Catholics, passing on our faith in the Lord's Real Presence in the Eucharist is our most precious gift and responsibility. That includes protecting our children's innocence and sense of wonder on every front in a hostile culture.

If we do not teach our children the truths of our faith, it only stands to reason that some other inferior or opposing "mystery" will fill the place that rightfully belongs to the one triune God. For the world is full of interesting gods all vying for attention, and ancient heresies that change fashionably to suit the particular confusions and temptations of every day and age. The New Age movement is, for the most part, a smorgasbord of some very old heresies.

In his **Letter to Families** written in 1994, the Year of the Family, Pope John Paul II makes the connection between the evangelizing role of the family and the Sacraments, especially the Eucharist. He acknowledges that the Apostles "came to understand that marriage and the family are a true vocation which comes from God himself and is an apostolate: the apostolate of the laity. Families are meant to contribute to the transformation of the earth and the renewal of the world, of creation and of all humanity." (**#18**)

The pope goes on to confirm that God's strength is "always far more powerful than your difficulties" in evangelizing, with the Sacraments of Reconciliation and Confirmation possessing "immeasurably greater" power than the evil at work in the world. "And incomparably greater than all is the power of the Eucharist." He continues, "The Eucharist is truly a wondrous sacrament . . . *It is for you, dear husbands and wives, parents and families!* Did Jesus not institute the Eucharist in a family-like setting during the Last Supper? When you meet for meals and are together in harmony, *Christ is close to you.* And he is Emmanuel, God with us, in an even greater way whenever you approach the table of the Eucharist . . . The Last Supper and the words he spoke there contain all the power and wisdom of the sacrifice of the cross. No other power and wisdom exist by which we can be saved and through which we can help to save others. There is no other power and no other wisdom by which you, parents, can educate both your children and yourselves. *The educational power of the Eucharist* has been proved down the generations and centuries." (*#18*)

Finally, Jesus makes it clear that only those who become as little children will enter the Kingdom of God (***Mark 10:13-16***). I think about my first embrace by the Lord Jesus and I know that in a mysterious way, children can love God in a special and undefended way — a way that many adults can no longer grasp for any number of reasons. Sometimes it is unfortunate that many people seem to define "growing up" as closing God out of their lives. But even if one were to take a lifetime detour in surrendering to the Lord, I believe that He will never cease to pursue us in the hope that we will come full-circle back to our spiritual childhood and recognize Him again, like the disciples on the road to Emmaus who recognized Jesus "in the breaking of the bread." (***Luke 24:35***)

Had no one ever told me about Jesus in the Eucharist I might never have been able to put a name to the One who loved me so much that day from the tabernacle. Although my life would have been changed, and I am sure I would have had some kind of a relationship with God, I could never have known the fullness of Love that I do as a Catholic Christian.

Childhood is a special opportunity, a "moment" when I believe that we need to tell our children about Jesus who loves us from the altar at every Mass because in a mysterious way we are allowed to be there with Him on the Cross. From that tiny "box" where His Real Presence remains, Jesus radiates an invitation and a challenge to embrace the indescribable love of our Father. He calls us to participate in and live the Eucharist. The whole Christian life flows from the pierced heart of Jesus, from which the Church was born (**Catechism of the Catholic Church, #766**), and His Sacred Heart is truly there for the taking with faith and love.

Armed with this incredible knowledge and faith, our children can someday answer the Lord's call to every Christian to go out into the entire world and proclaim the Gospel to all creatures (**Mark 16:15**). They will be able to do that because knowing how much God loves them can open their eyes to how much He loves us all, empowering them to serve *all* people in Jesus' name. We are called to change the world, to bring God's justice and peace to all nations.

CHAPTER 3

Adversary

St. Michael the Archangel, defend us in battle.
Be our safeguard against the wickedness and snares of the devil.
May God rebuke him, we humbly pray,
And do you, O prince of the heavenly host,
By the power of God, cast into hell Satan and all the evil spirits
Who prowl about the world seeking the ruin of souls.

Amen.

Pope Leo XIII

I learned at a very early age that the rest and peace of my
first encounter with the Lord Jesus are not the only reality
of life. Although it is the truest reality because Jesus has
conquered sin and death, we know from Scripture and consis-
tent Church teaching that there is evil in the world, and that
there are personal evil spirits whose miserable "job" it is to see
to it that we do not end up in heaven. St. Paul tells us that ". . .
we are not fighting against human beings but against the wicked
spiritual forces in the heavenly world" (*Eph. 6:12*). And so it
was very shortly after I met the Lord Jesus in His Eucharistic
Presence that He taught me that not only is there Someone
who loves me incomparably, but there is someone else who
hates me as well.

This episode in my life is not meant to frighten you. I
learned long ago not to question God's methods — that He
allows the enemy only what is necessary for the fulfillment of
His mysterious plan. I have also come to believe that sometimes
the Lord issues a "wake-up call" to us through the experience of

others, reminding us that we are, indeed, in a spiritual battle with eternal consequences, and to shake us out of our complacent denial of the reality of evil spirits. You must keep in mind that in His time, God gave me the grace to understand and deal with what you are about to read.

My mom had put me up to bed in my crib. I can still recall the footed pajamas I was wearing, and "see" the room I was in with its long windows and high, tin ceiling. It was dark but not pitch dark like nighttime in the country. A very large and bright street light stood on our Brooklyn corner, so despite blinds in the windows, light seeped through the slats anyway and it was never really dark in any of the rooms at night.

As a child I often seemed unready to go to bed when bedtime arrived. There were things to see. I still had lots of energy when I was put to bed most nights and I can recall this night very vividly, as well as the fact that I was not tired yet. That is why I was standing in the crib, just about tall enough to have my hands comfortably on the rail, hanging out with nothing to do. I might have been bouncing up and down. I did that sometimes to keep busy. What are crib mattresses for anyway?

As I stood there something started happening. In the far corner of the room what appeared to be a gossamer figure was forming — a smoky, wispy mask-like "face" of something very ugly and dark. I froze in place, grasping the railing, too little to have any idea what was going on. I remember experiencing a fear that I can never describe that gripped my heart like ice. It seemed like the room was freezing. I was shaking inside and outside. In retrospect I realize that I was experiencing pure hatred. It was my first encounter with Satan.

The "mask" looked like it was moving toward me very slowly and menacingly. The room seemed to grow darker as it drew closer. It recall that this dream-like image looked more animal than human, yet not like any animal I have ever seen. The most frightening part was the fear that was grasping my soul by now. I began to scream at the top of my lungs for my "mommy".

She burst into the room after what seemed like forever, and it was as if a light went on with her presence, even though I do not recall if she turned on the lights or not. What looked like a horrible "face" vanished as quickly as it had appeared. It had come quite close by the time she arrived. Between the sobs I tried to tell her about this thing in the room coming at me, and she smiled and reassured me over and over again that I was fine — that it was just a dream.

Although I will never know on this side of eternity just what happened for certain, as I grew older, I realized that this terrifying experience was somehow related to my powerful experience of Love, and in a very real sense, it grounded me for life. It left me with a clear intuition of what evil is and that intuition has never left me.

Although far from perfectly, to this day and to the best of my ability with the help of God's grace, I have tried not to waste time on anything that I knew was opposed to the light that is Christ. To do so is insanity. Sin is the only real insanity in the world, and I know, because even with the clear signs with which I was graced, I gave in to the very strong temptation to experiment briefly with the occult pracices of ouija boards and Tarot Cards when I was a teen and young adult.

I refused to believe that evil spirits could actually use them, but I was frightened away from them by the evil presence I experienced there. It was necessary for me, however, to explicitly renounce any involvement with these forbidden powers, and to seek the Lord's forgiveness in the Sacrament of Reconciliation for what Scripture clearly prohibits as a form of idolatry, which is what occult practices are (see *Catholic Catechism, # 2110-17*). I learned that there is no casual involvement with the occult as some insist ("Oh, I just read the astrology column for fun. I don't really believe in it.") I have observed over the years that all the evil one needs is a small psychic "opening" to mysteriously gain a foothold into our spiritual lives and begin to distort them. I believe that he can and does use it to draw us away from God individually, and then creates global chaos, one person at a time, helping to fuel grave evils like abortion, terrorism, genocide, prejudice, wars, murder and euthanasia. I believe that is a topic that needs to be taken very seriously and developed further.

As I look back as an adult it seems to me that the evil one does himself a disservice in making himself so obvious, and that is probably why he does not do it so often. For the most part, I have discerned his activity as being most fruitful when he patiently chips away at our faith, weakening us and using our own weaknesses against us, and then going in for the kill. Our own time is cursed especially in that works of darkness have been accepted as good; the forces of evil have even managed to pull generations of Christians and people of good faith away from simple common sense. For wisdom is a gift of the Holy Spirit and when darkness reigns, wisdom disappears (***Wisdom 9:6***). We live in a technologically insane world today. It seems as if Satan really was given the last century to try to destroy the family, youth and the priesthood, but he cannot succeed.

In retrospect I realize that my first taste of hell graced me with wisdom beyond my years and filled me with a great respect for the power of evil, but even more so, an appreciation for the power of God that infinitely surpasses the devil's power. That is really quite obvious because God is the Creator to Whom the devil owes his existence. Jesus has broken the enemy's power for those who accept Him as Lord and Savior. Jesus has set us free if we choose to accept the gift.

Scripture and Church teaching have affirmed throughout the ages that we are indeed fighting a battle with evil spirits who are real, spiteful and powerful. It was this horrendous fear that Our Lord conquered by His death on the Cross. It was the power of death itself that Jesus banished in the power of His Resurrection. He dispels the power of the evil one when the Holy Spirit comes into our lives, particularly at Baptism when we become God's adopted children and are set free from Satan's curse.

The ***Catechism of the Catholic Church*** (***#395***) explains that the work of the devil is to lead men to disobey God.

> The power of Satan is, nonetheless, not infinite. He is only a creature, powerful from the fact that he is pure spirit, but still a creature. He cannot prevent the building up of God's reign. Although Satan may act in the world out of hatred for God and his kingdom in Christ Jesus, and although his action may cause grave injuries — of a spiritual nature and, indirectly, even of a physical nature — to each man and to society, the action is permitted by divine providence which with strength and gentleness guides human and cosmic history. It is a great mystery that providence should permit diabolical activity, but 'we know that in everything God works for good for those who love him.' (***Rom. 8:28***)

Most of the time, I've observed the works of Satan to be subtle and very cunning. Yet I do not think many people can deny the depths of evil that humanity can sink to, the hellish acts of which we are capable. Simply look at Adolph Hitler's horrible legacy and the diabolical acts of Islamic terrorists in murdering thousands of innocent civilians on Sept. 11, 2001 in the United States, for example. For many poor souls that hell seems to begin on earth, perhaps because we sometimes refuse to acknowledge the truth of evil and spend our lives running from its remedy. There is a grace waiting there for us. And there is someone who can help us face the reality of life and to give our lives to her divine Son.

As I think about that experience in my room, I smile when I recall that the first person I called for was my mother. The natural response of a baby is to call her mother or father. I see the parallel between my mom and Mary, my spiritual mother, very clearly in this experience. For it is Mary who crushes the head of the serpent, whose power over the evil one is great in her role as Mother of the Incarnate Word whose *fiat* shared in the beginning of the work of redemption for us all.

Although I did not make this connection until years later, I thank God also for the gift of His mother, who is our mother in faith. God has given us a "mommy" to call when we are as frightened as little children by the wickedness and snares of the devil, and she will always come to our aid and lead us to her Son.

CHAPTER 4

The Holy Spirit

Come Holy Spirit
fill the hearts of your faithful,
and enkindle in them the fire of your Love.
Send forth your spirit
and they shall be created
and you shall renew the face of the earth.
Traditional Prayer

I grew up in Williamsburg, Brooklyn, in a blue-collar, mixed factory and residential area. My dad owned a restaurant and bar, and my family lived in the house built above the business. The cook's name was Freddie and I used to love the way he prepared his London broil, so my sisters and I often ate lunch downstairs with the factory workers who were my dad's faithful lunch crowd. I was always fascinated by the pinball machine in the bar.

Sometime between receiving the Lord in my first Communion and receiving the Sacrament of Confirmation, I remember wondering about the Holy Spirit. At that time, we called Him the "Holy Ghost" and I thought that was kind of spooky. We had been introduced to the Holy Spirit in the Scriptures where He descended on Jesus in the form of a dove, and that gentle image was comforting to me.

Still, as I approached Confirmation I wanted to know more about this "ghost" who would be coming to me in a new way, leaving an indelible mark on my soul. Inwardly, I was praying to know more about Him. The Jesus I knew was the most gentle person I had ever met. If this Spirit was His Spirit, He had to be okay.

Our factory neighborhood was definitely not pretty. The trucks rumbled by the house day in and day out, spewing their exhaust and soot into the air constantly. The machinery-making plant down the street added some louder noise to the picture. And just about the only birds we ever saw were the dingy sparrows and the shades-of-gray pigeons.

Several people in the neighborhood had pigeon coops on their roofs and would let their flocks out to exercise most days. The birds stayed together as their owners directed their flight patterns by raising a long pole and moving it in the direction they wanted the birds to fly.

As best as I can recall, one sunny day my dad called me downstairs to see something he had to show me. I raced downstairs as quickly as I could because he had been so mysterious about just why I had to come immediately. What I saw when I walked into the building was a complete surprise.

I can still see my father smiling with a beautiful snow-white dove sitting very calmly on his arm. I was delighted but puzzled at the same time. What was a dove doing in our neighborhood? With all the pigeons around, I had never, ever seen a dove except in books or in the zoo.

Dad told me to put out my arm and I did so a bit hesitantly, but at the same time I was quivering inside with excitement. This wondrous creature walked over onto my skinny little arm, completely calm, undisturbed by our presence. It was beautifully white, an almost impossible feat for a pure white dove in a dirty city neighborhood. And although I knew that the Holy Spirit was not a bird, I could not help but think about the Holy Spirit to whom I had been praying for some time.

As the thought of the Holy Spirit descending in the form of a dove over Jesus during His Baptism crossed my mind, my own "fear" of the Holy Spirit just melted away. In what I know now to be a moment of grace, I recognized the Love that I was experiencing while thinking about the Holy Spirit as that very same Love that had touched me from the tabernacle several years before, when I was very young.

It was the very same Love that I treasured so much the first time I received Jesus in the Eucharist, and every time I've celebrated and received Jesus in the Eucharist since then. It was the Love of every prayer and every hug; how could I be afraid of the Holy "Ghost"? The word did not do Him any justice and I was delighted when "Holy Spirit" came into use with the second Vatican Council.

When the dove became too heavy for me to carry anymore, I was forced to put it down on the nearest horizontal surface, which happened to be the pinball machine. Incredibly, it walked around entirely unafraid of any of us, ultimately coming back to me. I was fascinated for some time, especially by its lack of any fear and its elegant grace. What beautiful creatures doves are, and what a perfect image for the Spirit of all holiness!

I don't know what became of our lovely visitor after I went back upstairs. My father died more than 30 years ago and I never asked him. He probably let it go free outside, hoping it would find its way home.

But I will always wonder exactly where home was. In all the years I had observed birds in the sky, I had never seen a white dove highlighted in a flock of pigeons, circling above a tarred Brooklyn rooftop. And I never did see one again until I saw that delicate white dove walking on Route 80 in the Delaware Water Gap just a few years ago.

Although I will never know where that beautiful creature came from, over the years I have come to see that one thing is for certain. God arranged the situation to teach me more about Himself in a way that both delighted me as a child and opened me to His grace.

After this experience, I could never again think of the Spirit of God as a "ghost" with all the negative connotations of death attached to that word. I could only think of Him in terms of gentleness, love and life.

I already knew the love of Jesus in the Blessed Sacrament, and now I had connected that love with the Holy Spirit. As a result of this "lesson", I was ready to accept His coming to me in Confirmation in a deeper way without childish fears. The Holy Spirit was already coming upon me, preparing me, and I was very grateful, even then.

A brief explanation of the symbol of the dove used for the Holy Spirit appears in Part I of the ***Catechism of the Catholic Church (# 701)***.

The dove. At the end of the flood, whose symbolism refers to Baptism, a dove released by Noah returns with a fresh olive-tree branch in its beak as a sign that the earth was again habitable.* When Christ comes up from the water of his baptism, the Holy Spirit, in the form of a dove, comes down upon him and remains with him.** The Spirit comes down and remains in the purified hearts of the baptized. In certain churches, the Eucharist is reserved in a metal receptacle in the form of a dove *(columbarium)* suspended above the altar. Christian iconography traditionally uses a dove to suggest the Spirit.

* Cf. *Gen* 8:8-12.

** Cf. *Mt* 3:16 and parallels.

As I reflect further on this memory, I find it delightful that it was my father who gave me the dove. After all, Jesus and the Holy Spirit are the gift of God the Father to us. **The Catholic Catechism** teaches that "when the Father sends his Word, he always sends his Breath. In their joint mission, the Son and the Holy Spirit are distinct but inseparable. To be sure, it is Christ who is seen, the visible image of the invisible God, but it is the Spirit who reveals him" (**# 689**).

In his encyclical letter **The Holy Spirit in the Life of the Church and the World**, Pope John Paul II brings his reflections on "the breath of divine life, the Holy Spirit" (**Part 3, No. 6: 65**) to a close by teaching that the simplest and most common way that the Holy Spirit is experienced is in prayer, helping us in our weakness (**Rom. 8:26**).

It was through a prayerful moment in the power of the Holy Spirit that I was graced to experience His love and better understand Who He is. The Lord used a lovely part of our everyday world as a "visual aid" to open my heart to this personal revelation. And I was delighted.

Although I was a good student and played a great deal of sports when I was a child, the Lord drew me to prayer daily. I got to Mass more often than just Sundays, and daily during Advent and Lent. I made time for Him throughout each day, even if it was just for a short visit to church to spend some quiet time with Him in the Blessed Sacrament, or by praying a Rosary in my room.

I believe that if we commit ourselves to a daily time of prayer, and if we ask the Lord that we might come to know Him better, we will certainly receive what we pray for. And that goes for our children in a special way. Jesus loves the prayers of little children and calls us all to have childlike hearts (***Mark 10:13***).

The Lord really does work in marvelous and mysterious ways, meeting us wherever we need to meet Him in order to be taught by Him, even if that is on a pinball machine in a factory neighborhood in Brooklyn. And He delights in delighting us.

CHAPTER 5

Confirmation

Sequence for Pentecost

Holy Spirit, Lord of Light,
From Thy throne in splendor bright
Shed on us a ray divine;
Come and from Thy boundless store
On our hearts Thy treasures pour;
Come and make us truly Thine.
O thou blessed light divine,
Shine within these hearts of Thine,
And our inmost being fill!
Heal our wounds, our strength renew;
On our dryness pour Thy dew;
Wash our stains of guilt away.
Bend and sway our stubborn will;
From our hearts remove the chill;
Guide our footsteps when we stray.

Traditional Prayer

The day of my Confirmation, Oct. 26, 1958, arrived at last and I remember the anticipation and excitement I experienced. I was only in the sixth grade. Despite my nervousness, I found my attention turning to the Holy Spirit even in the confusion of preparations and all the little details that seem to loom large when any significant ceremony approaches.

It became hard to focus on anything but the Holy Spirit as I entered the church. I remember almost nothing about the ceremony itself. Like so many of my classmates, I was concerned that the bishop was going to "tap" me too hard. Back in pre-Vatican II days, the bishop gave each young man and woman a light pat on the face — so the Sisters told us — as a reminder that we must have the courage to defend our faith.

I can still see myself kneeling before the bishop, nervous about the least important part of the entire Sacrament. As it turned out, however, the bishop's "tap" was a bit stronger than I had expected. I think he did not realize how tiny I was and I was a bit suprised. It made me wonder about the difficulties of defending one's faith.

What I remember most clearly are the effects of the Sacrament that I experienced. As I returned to my pew, I was filled with a joy that was so rich and so overpowering that I wanted to laugh and sing and cry all at once. I simply cannot describe this kind of joy. To a lesser degree it had always been present any time I prayed. It had especially flooded my soul after Mass or Benediction or prayers before the Blessed Sacrament. But now it was overwhelming and it brought with it a deep sense of peace and a powerful love that filled me with a strong desire to do anything that God wanted of me. I knew that I belonged only to Him.

In addition to these amazing effects, I *knew* that if I laid my hands on the sick and prayed in Jesus' name, people could be healed. In fact, I had a strong desire to do just that. I knew that it was possible for God to work miracles, real miracles, through me. And I thought I had lost my mind.

No one had ever told me that there are more than seven gifts of the Holy Spirit. I had no idea that there were charismatic gifts in addition to the gifts of wisdom, knowledge, understanding, fortitude, counsel, piety and fear of the Lord known as the Isaiah gifts because of their location in ***Isaiah 11:2-3*** — that there are charismatic gifts given for the building up of the Body of Christ here on earth, gifts for evangelization to empower Christians to go out to all the world and tell the Good News. But the Holy Spirit knew and He poured them out on me.

I didn't know what to do with them. I was only 10 years old and there was no support system in place for me. As time went on, I gradually lost my zeal to pray over people. But I never forgot about being an instrument for healing prayer, about wanting to shout from the rooftops that Jesus is Lord — that He really is God and He really loves us. Despite the fact that I did not even have names for the gifts that I had been empowered with, at least not until many years later, I knew inwardly that they were from the Holy Spirit. I recognized the Love that accompanies them.

So these remarkable gifts simply went to sleep in me, below the surface, waiting until the day when the Spirit would bring them back to my consciousness again. And although I did not use these gifts fully, I remembered them. The charismatic gifts of the Holy Spirit — healing, prophecy, teaching, miracles, word of knowledge, discernment, tongues and the interpretation of tongues — were a promise of wonderful things to come back to the surface when the Church itself would begin to reawaken to these gifts of the Holy Spirit which empower believers for service.

The graces of the charismatic gifts of the Holy Spirit have existed in the life of the Church since Pentecost and St. Paul names them in *1 Corinthians 12: 1-11.* The **Catechism of the Catholic Church** describes these graces:

> Grace is first and foremost the gift of the Spirit who justifies and sanctifies us. But grace also includes the gifts that the Spirit grants us to associate us with his work, to enable us to collaborate in the salvation of others and in the growth of the Body of Christ, the Church. There are *sacramental graces*, gifts proper to the different sacraments. There are furthermore *special graces*, also called *charisms*, after the Greek term used by St. Paul and meaning 'favor', 'gratuitous gift,' 'benefit.'* Whatever their character — sometimes it is extraordinary, such as the gift of miracles or tongues — charisms are oriented toward sanctifying grace and are intended for the common good of the Church. They are at the service of charity which builds up the Church.** (*#2003*)
>
> * Cf. *LG* 12.
>
> ** Cf. *1 Cor.* 12.

There can be great witnessing power in a healing or miracle worked in the name of Jesus to bring some people to the faith, and to affirm the faith of the believer in Jesus.

Very importantly, the love and joy that I had received when Jesus touched me from the tabernacle now seemed to multiply and to pervade my every moment in a completely surprising way. And a marvelous peace settled deeply into my soul. I watched that same awesome peace bless each of my children immediately after their own Confirmations.

Over the years, I learned how to recognize the gifts of the Holy Spirit at work in me. It became easier to realize when the Spirit was leading me in His very gentle ways, but usually in retrospect. I found that the presence of the gifts of the Holy Spirit made it possible for me to trust the Lord more and more in all the details of my life because He always came through. For the most part these inspirations of the Spirit came very quietly and they came over many, many years.

I learned through what I call baby steps — by being obedient when it seemed as if the Spirit was inspiring me to pray, or to work on changing a bad habit, or to be faithful to my commitment to Sunday Mass even when I was being tempted to stay in bed later, for example. Often I find these little challenges to be much harder than the great trials we encounter, because they are so frequent and relentless that we are broken down by their monotony and never reach the spiritual goal we are seeking. We might not even realize that we are no longer seeking God.

In retrospect, I realize that it is the Spirit that breaks the monotony by bringing new life into every moment lived for God. Because of the presence of the Spirit's gifts, I see that I seemed to become more docile to the working of the Spirit during times of difficulty when I could have given up on my faith, or settled for a watered down version of it. The divine gift of fortitude was evident here. I learned much about divine patience and divine anger and divine forgiveness during my teen years, more often by returning to the Lord in the Sacrament of Reconciliation when I had stubbornly or stupidly failed Him by being just the "littlest bit" dishonest or unkind or disobedient to His Word and the teachings of the Church.

It was always through the Sacrament of Reconciliation that I felt a new rush of the divine breath of the Spirit, a renewed strength, as I still do today. The Lord taught me constantly as I gave in to the Spirit's inspiration to read spiritual books and writings of the saints that helped me understand what growing in the faith means — and watching the fruits of the Spirit — love, joy, peace, patience, kindness, goodness, faithfulness, gentleness and self-control — grow as well. Divine wisdom, counsel and understanding helped me make good life decisions. As I trusted and saw how good it is to follow the Lord, it became easier to obey His Word the next time.

When I was a young adult, the Lord arranged through some interesting circumstances for me to surrender more deeply to Him and I "found" the charismatic gifts again. I speak of this encounter in detail in Chapter 17, "Lessons in the Darkness."

All the graces of my Confirmation welled up in my soul once more. I welcomed them back within a Church community that now supported these gifts. I realized that part of the overwhelming joy I had experienced so many years ago after my Confirmation included the gift of tongues, which I now yielded to as an adult. Believe me, I was most surprised by it! I felt as if I had finally become "whole" in the Holy Spirit. It seemed as if I had gone full circle, traveling all the way into adulthood only to find spiritual childhood again. It was wonderful.

Over the years, I have encountered several people who related similar experiences to my own when they were confirmed in Christ. And I thank the Holy Spirit, the Spirit of Jesus and the Father, for moving so powerfully in all of our lives, even when we do not recognize that until many years later.

The Holy Spirit is and has always been at work in the Church since its "birthday" on Pentecost. Yet every time has its particular graces and needs. In so many authentic renewal movements in our own time, God Himself seems to be appropriating abundant graces publicly upon His sometimes sleeping Church as the pure gifts that they are. People seem to be "awakening" to the spiritual life in new movements growing within the universal Church. From personal experience, I've come to see that the charismatic renewal is a valuable school in the area of charisms today, having proclaimed and promoted the release to these graces for more than 30 years. But those graces were poured upon me in Baptism, and took conscious root when I was only a nervous 10-year-old kneeling before a bishop in Brooklyn, receiving the Sacrament of Confirmation, firmly planted in the heart of the Church.

The special work of the Spirit — the purpose of all of the gifts of the Holy Spirit — is unity in love. It is the Spirit who is the soul of the Church, the marvelous gift that Jesus left us to bring us into unity.

Many a time, I watched a single burning coal go out quickly when removed from the rest of the coals in a fire in our coal stove. Just as with the coals, so it is with us. When we are together, the Holy Spirit can move more readily and easily burn brightly in us.

For that fire to blaze and ignite others most powerfully, it only stands to reason that we need to allow all the graces of our Confirmation to emerge and grow in our lives. We need all the gifts of the Holy Spirit to evangelize a dark and dying world, for the New Evangelization envisioned by Pope John Paul II.

We must take the Sacrament of Confirmation seriously, and never grieve the Holy Spirit by saying "no" to Him. If we allow the Holy Spirit to empower us, if we say "yes" to His power and Presence as did our mother in faith, Mary, then we will not only daily grow in love for the Church, our spiritual shelter and home, but many people will flock to find that joy in the Church, set on fire with God's Love as well.

Come Holy Spirit!

Our Father

O ur Father,

Who art in heaven,

Hallowed be Your name.

Your kingdom come.

Your will be done on earth

as it is in heaven.

Give us this day our daily

bread, and

Forgive us our trespasses

As we forgive those who

trespass against us,

And lead us not into

temptation,

But deliver us from evil.

Amen.

When I was a teenager, my friend Barbara and I used to "hang out" on school nights at Joe's Candy Store on Metropolitan Avenue in our Brooklyn neighborhood. She and I were inseparable when we were in St. Joseph's High School in downtown Brooklyn, and we traveled to school together on the public bus every day. My curfew was 10 p.m. on school nights. I have to admit that I often stretched curfew and came home late; my grades were good and we were having such fun that it was hard to go home. Sometimes my mom and dad would already be in bed upstairs when I had come home.

This particular night was a typical school night. Barbara and I had spent our usual evening with the rest of the teenagers who hung out at Joe's. I remember it being pretty chilly outside that night. I was late again getting home and hoping against hope that my mother was already asleep. When I tiptoed into the kitchen, the first room upon entering our house after climbing the long, curved staircase to the second floor, I gave a sigh of relief. She was, indeed, asleep. I could grab a bedtime snack and do the same.

As I started out across the kitchen, I was all at once aware of God's Presence so powerfully that I literally stopped in my tracks. I found myself unable to move from the spot where I stood, transfixed. My knees were so weak that I had to lean against the nearest wall to remain standing. Nothing like this had ever happened to me before and I did not know what to do, but I was not in the least bit frightened.

The Presence of the Lord was so awesome and powerful that the entire room seemed to fill up with Him, almost making the air heavy and difficult to breathe. The whole room was permeated with love, a love that commanded the most profound reverence and adoration, a love that was majestic and filled me with wonder. I was overwhelmed by the Lord, taken by such surprise that I literally could not even think.

I don't remember how long it was before I could gather my thoughts or speak. But when I finally regained some sense of where I was and what was happening, I found myself asking the Lord out loud, "What do you want, Lord?" I think that had an entire room full of people been present, I would not have noticed them. God had captured my complete attention and I surrendered to His invitation to pray, in whatever way He wanted me to do that.

I began to pray the **Our Father**, but as I had never prayed it before. **The Our Father** is a prayer that I had come to take very much for granted. I spoke the words audibly, unable to rattle them off like I was used to when reciting prayers in a group, or when reciting a Rosary. Every word seemed to overflow with meanings which I needed to absorb and take to heart.

Our Father, who art in heaven, hallowed be Thy name. I had to stop and simply soak up the holiness of God the Father, and just "be" with Him for a while. When I could move on I finished the prayer, slowly thinking about each phrase, adoring the Father constantly. It was the incredible holiness and majesty of God that had captured me that night, entirely by surprise.

When I came to the close of the prayer, "*And lead us not into temptation, but deliver us from evil. Amen,*" I knew the protection of God from all that would harm me. And I experienced the loving embrace of God as Father, all powerful in His forgiveness and gentleness and mercy all at once. I could never be afraid of my heavenly Father. All I could do was love Him and know that despite difficulties in life, He is my all powerful Lord who would protect me through anything I would ever encounter, and I need not be afraid of anything as long as I have Him.

I couldn't move for a long time. It seemed to last forever. I closed my eyes and just continued to lean against the wall for support. And when I finally opened my eyes, I could only wonder: What was that all about? Why had the Lord chosen to love me so powerfully *this* very ordinary night? My mind was not focusing on prayer at all; I had not even been praying. But again the Lord clearly taught me that it is He who chooses us, not we who choose Him, and He chooses to choose us in *His* time, not ours.

I believe that Jesus, in the power of His Spirit, was saying the prayer with me that night, because I experienced such love for God the Father that I knew it was Jesus' own love for Him. It was the love of someone who knew His Father well, someone who would be willing to die for Him.

I realize now that when we pray the ***Our Father*** with Jesus, we are sharing in the very life of God in the Trinity in a very affectionate and personal way as an adopted daughter or son. **The Catechism of the Catholic Church** explains it thus:

> We can invoke God as Father because *he is revealed to us* by his Son become man and because his Spirit makes him known to us . . .
>
> When we pray to the Father, we are *in communion with him* and with his Son, Jesus Christ.* Then we know and recognize him with an ever new sense of wonder. *(#2780-81)*
>
> * Cf. *1 Jn* 1:3.

The grace of sharing Jesus' love for our "Abba" (**Gal. 4:6**) has remained with me since that evening and, hopefully, has grown. That is because every single time that we pray the prayer that Jesus Himself taught us, we are living in a graced moment. The most powerful lesson of that night was, I believe, that we *always* pray with Jesus to our Father in the power of the Holy Spirit. Occasionally we might be aware of that but what we feel has little to do with what is happening in faith.

I wish I could say that I have always prayed as fervently as I did that night because I have not. I wish I could say that I never took the prayer to our Father that Jesus gave us lightly again, because I have. But the memory of that night has made me more aware when I was failing to put my own heart, my own love, into Jesus' prayer for and with us to our Father. I consider this a great grace.

I "met" God my Father in a very personal way that night in the kitchen of my childhood home on Berry Street in Brooklyn, and I loved Him. I have allowed God to care for me ever since I experienced His love as a baby, and can honestly say that I have never experienced a sense of anxiety about anything in this life. Trials, worries and hurts have come, but in the deepest part of my spirit there is a peace that defies all description that was born over the first few years of my life, when all three Persons of the Blessed Trinity were introduced to me. In the **Our Father** we are all given access to the life of God in an intimate way in faith.

I grow daily in my understanding of the depth of this perfect prayer and I will never get it completely right, but I can try. What began that night has been a constant teaching over many, many years as the Holy Spirit continues to enlighten my mind in the ordinary, "uneventful" days that make up the bulk of my life. I placed that word in quotes because I believe that simply being alive is enough to make a day eventful. I look forward to further lessons.

Above all, since that night I have been absolutely certain in faith of the mercy and gentleness of God the Father, who cares for us, His tiny, frail children, in every little detail. We need to give God permission to teach us to pray whenever and however He chooses. We need to let Him have His way in our lives, as did Mary, the mother of God, the perfect model of trust and faith.

CHAPTER 7

Sleds, Coal Bins and Angels

Angel of God, my guardian dear,
to whom God's Love commits me here,
ever this day be at my side
to light and guard, to rule and guide. Amen.
Traditional prayer

When I was young, my parents would occasionally visit friends who lived outside New York City. Although I was a city kid, I never liked living in the city and so I looked forward to the days when we would drive up to Connecticut or New York State, or out to New Jersey. Sunday was usually our traveling day. We took our road trips winter, spring, summer and fall.

This particular winter weekend, my parents drove us all out of state on a Sunday afternoon to visit with some friends and their children. I don't recall how old I was. I know I was still in grade school. There was snow on the ground, and there was a great sledding hill near the home of the people we were visiting. My sisters and I must have taken turns borrowing a sled from the couple's children, since I do not recall bringing any with us, and enjoyed the afternoon sliding down the hill.

A good sledding hill can become crowded quickly. Before we knew it, it seemed as if the whole neighborhood was barreling down the hill along with us. It never dawned on me that too many children on a hill could add up to a dangerous situation. Being a city kid, this was probably one of my first experiences with so much space to play on. Sledding in the middle of Brooklyn is very different from sledding in the country.

On one of my trips down the hill, as I came nearer to the bottom, I became uncomfortable with the speed I was flying at and dragged my feet to slow the sled down. I was not aware of any danger at that point. In fact, I do not recall hearing anyone

yelling to warn me that another sled was about to run over me.

It's possible I just didn't hear any warning cries if they existed, because as a city kid, I did not expect to hear them. But without understanding why, as my sled was rolling to a stop, I sensed that I should roll myself over sideways onto the snow. It certainly did not make any sense but I rolled over anyway, although I took my time about it.

As I did so, I felt another sled speed by me so quickly and so close to me that it actually grazed my snow pants, almost tearing them. I was shocked and found myself shaking at the close call that I had experienced. I do not think that the boy who had almost run me over even looked back. All in a day's sledding, I guess.

But I shuddered at the thought of what my leg might have looked like had his sled collided with me at that speed. The wood and metal sleds of my childhood were heavy duty models and the runners became weapons when they were moving at any speed.

I sat on the snow shaking for a few minutes, aware that I could have been badly injured or even crippled in a split second. I sensed that I had been protected from this injury, and I hope I had the sense to thank God for inspiring me to move out of harm's way. I certainly thank Him now. I walked up the hill with my sled, moved to a less crowded part of the hill and continued to sled. I think if I had not, I might not ever have had the nerve to sled again. In fact, now I move faster down snow-covered mountains rather than hills. My favorite sport is downhill skiing.

When I was a child, I used to love the prayer card depicting the angel guarding two young children crossing a bridge. That prayer card was a favorite of my daughter Mary Beth when she was young as well. I also loved the prayer to my guardian angel, a devotion that was consoling and beautiful.

Especially after that afternoon of sledding, I believed that I really did have an angel who lovingly protected me from harm. But I appreciated it much more as I grew up and understood more fully the enormous consequences that a serious accident on that day could have had on the rest of my life.

Many years later, as a young mother of three, my belief in

guardian angels was powerfully confirmed another cold winter day. My family heated our New Jersey home for some years with a coal stove, and near the garage stood a coal bin which held a ton of coal. I would trudge out to the bin and bring in hods of coal throughout the day to keep the fire going.

Resembling a lean-to shed, the coal bin had a heavy, shingled black roof which would have to be lifted and propped up carefully with a two by four — and I emphasize carefully —in order to reach the coal inside the bin. I had great respect for that roof. It weighed at least 40 pounds, almost half my own weight, and after I had wedged the two by

four between the edge of the bin and the roof, I always checked to see that it was stable. It was entirely safe if I was careful, and until this day, I had made it a point to be very cautious.

However, this particular day I was in a hurry. I shoved the

two by four in place quickly and stuck my head into the bin. The coal level was fairly low, so I had to lean quite a way into it. I did not bother to check whether the two by four was in place correctly.

Without warning, the two by four gave way and the roof came down squarely on my neck and back. But as it hit me I felt absolutely nothing. It was as if someone was holding it up, because there was no pain and no pressure at all. I was not only able to pull myself out of the way of the roof, which is quite impossible since it should have pinned me in place, but when I reached for it, it felt as light as a feather!

Shaking again as I had as a child when the sled missed my leg by a fraction of an inch, I knew once again the amazing protection of the Lord in the comforting existence of His angels. I cannot express how fervently I thanked Him this time, not just for this particular blessing, but also for all the times He has protected me and I have not known it.

Over the years, I have heard about many more encounters from friends and acquaintances during which they were protected from injury or even death in remarkable ways. I have come to truly believe that I, too, was protected when the sled nearly ripped my leg open and when the coal bin roof could have broken my back.

The Catholic Church has always taught that the existence of angels is a truth witnessed to by Scripture and tradition, although we cannot know exactly how it all works.

Scripture tells us,

> For God commands the angels
> to guard you in all your ways. *(Psalm 91:11)*

Along with St. Basil who is quoted in the **Catholic Cat-echism (#336**), "Beside each believer stands an angel as protector and shepherd leading him to life" * St. Basil, *Adv. Eunonium III,* 1: PG 29, 656B, I have come to know that guardian angels exist. To this day I remain completely amazed at the incredible ways that I have been protected from harm despite my stupidity. I still think of these experiences with complete astonishment and thanksgiving to God and to my guardian angel.

It is unfortunate that there are so many confusing and erroneous theories today about the nature of angels. Some seem to believe that people can become angels after they die. That is quite impossible; angels are angels and human beings are human beings. We are both created by our Father but we are different.

We do not work towards becoming our "angel selves" either. Scripture recalls angels sometimes appearing in human form and that is a mystery. But some TV shows and movies have portrayed angels in silly and even sacrilegious ways, where "angels" fall in love and act like fallen human beings. The devil loves confusion, which is why he apparently never grows tired of sowing so many seeds of confusion in human minds. An informed and strong faith is the only way to discern the spiritual counterfeits. And the real thing is so wonderful there is no need for counterfeits.

I learned a valuable lesson from the combination of these two experiences. I learned that God's protection remains with us always, even when we do dumb things. And taking that a bit further, I learned that the Father's protection is especially strong when things *do not* seem to be going our way, or when God seems to be playing hide and seek with us.

We don't have to feel it; we just have to believe it and our faith in Jesus opens the door to the Lord's action. When we pray "Deliver us from evil" in the **Our Father**, God truly answers at just the moment we need it.

It's a wonderful, consoling thought that according to God's will, these powerful and holy angels who constantly behold the face of the living God and serve as His messengers are helping us on our journey through this life. It is good to remember and thank them, giving glory to God for His providence at all times.

CHAPTER 8

A Helping Hand

Lord, I am not worthy to receive you,
but only say the word, and I shall be healed.
Traditional Prayer before Communion

When I learned the above prayer as a child before Vatican Council II, it ended with the words "and my soul shall be healed." The Council reaffirmed the Church's constant teaching that for we human beings made up of body, mind and spirit (or soul), the body too participates in the healing of the soul, and will participate ultimately in the general resurrection of the dead at the end of time.

So the wording of that prayer generally changed after the Council to a broader understanding of God's all inclusive healing power, that "I" shall be healed. Salvation extends to our bodies as well as our souls.

One winter evening many years ago, the Lord decided to show me how His healing power extends to all of me. Our dear friends Maureen and Ralph Cure hosted a home Mass. It was a small, informal group of friends who played together in our parish folk group and prayer group, coming together around the Lord's table.

Despite the fact that I would have loved to play guitar, I could not. Every winter I was plagued with terribly dry skin on my hands, which caused a condition where my fingertips developed deep and painful cuts. This evening, several of my fingers were hurting pretty badly. Although I usually wrapped up my fingers in Band Aids with antibiotic ointment to facilitate healing, I chose not to do so tonight because I felt that all those bandaged fingers would have drawn too much attention.

Other than the fact of its home setting there was nothing unusual to mark this Mass over and above any other daily Mass. Yet sometime after the consecration, I recall looking down at my hands, possibly because I felt less pain. What I saw happening literally took my breath away.

At a clearly accelerated speed, the deep cuts in my fingers were closing up right before my eyes. Perhaps the best description I can give is time-lapse photography of flowers. When the speed is increased during playback of a film of flowers' movements, which we cannot perceive but can be recorded by a camera, we become aware of the dance that flowers perform all the time. Healing of these deep cuts usually takes days of treatment for me. Yet I was witnessing it happening almost immediately, like the accelerated viewing of dancing flowers.

At first I didn't believe it. I tried to pay attention to what was happening during Eucharist but I had to look down again. As I did, I pulled on Steve's shirtsleeve and whispered as calmly as I could (which was not too calmly) to look at my fingers. Within what I would estimate to be no more than two minutes, every split in every finger had closed and healed and all the pain had disappeared.

Steve and I both were amazed. Without my asking for healing Jesus had done so in a very gracious and surprising way,

I believe, so that we might learn more about Him.

This experience taught me two things that are etched in my memory: the healing power of *every* celebration of Eucharist on many levels, and the loving, healing initiative of the Lord Jesus. On what was a very ordinary night during a very simple home Mass in which I was very distracted by the throbbing in my fingertips, all I had to do was to *be* there as best as I could, open to Jesus and whatever He would choose to do.

Nothing is impossible for God and God is present in the tremendous healing power of Jesus completely present in the Eucharist —His Body and Blood, soul and divinity as we Catholics were taught so very many years ago. The Lord let me actually watch my fingers heal in an impossibly short time span and convinced me that the power of just being at Mass, of being in His Eucharistic Presence, is so great that anything can be made whole, without even asking. I tremble when I think that we receive Jesus' Sacred Heart personally every time that we receive Him in Communion. I have never stopped meditating on that.

It seems that before the Council the focus on physical healing is difficult to find in Church teaching, documents and practice, except for the great shrines like Lourdes, where many medically certified miracles have been confirmed, and through people who were known as healers, like Capuchin Franciscan Father Solanus Casey, whom God used to perform thousands of confirmed healings. But the Council seems to have been a turning point which brought the message of healing that is at the very heart of the Gospel back into focus on a universal scale.

In the Scriptures, Jesus spends the majority of His ministry in healing the sick in spirit, mind and body. And Jesus charges His Church to do the same. In *Mt. 10:8,* Jesus commands the first Apostles to give without cost what they have received without cost, teaching that the Kingdom of Heaven "is at hand." He admonishes them to "cure the sick, raise the dead, cleanse lepers and drive out demons." Over the centuries, the Church has reached out to serve the sick and the poor in countless ways through countless people.

That is because "[the Church] believes in the life-giving presence of Christ, the physician of souls and bodies. This presence is particularly active through the sacraments, and in an altogether special way through the Eucharist, the bread that gives eternal life and that St. Paul suggests is connected with bodily health," * Cf. *Jn* 6:54, 58; 1 *Cor* 11:30, the **Catechism of the Catholic Church** points out (*#1509*). My small healing related in this chapter is a testimony to that.

The Church also acknowledges a special charism of healing given to some " . . . so as to make manifest the power of the grace of the risen Lord" (**CC, #1508**). Within the Catholic Charismatic Renewal, the gift of healing is welcomed and practiced, with marvelous "signs and wonders" to the glory of God occurring throughout the world in the power of the Holy Spirit. The contribution made by the renewal to this compassionate ministry is enormous. The Lord has raised up men and women gifted with the healing charism, and many prayer groups have a healing ministry which ministers to anyone who has need of prayer. It is a grace for the whole Church and every one of its members, most especially in helping all to realize that the healing charism is the grace of the entire Church.

Although it remains a mystery as to why the Lord seems to choose to heal some and not others, the catechism reminds us that even St. Paul was taught by Our Lord that " . . . my grace is sufficient for you, for my power is made perfect in weakness" (*2 Cor. 12:9*). There are many levels and kinds of healing, and I believe that no true prayer said with faith and humility goes unanswered. If we trust in our Lord, we come to understand that His Will is perfect and that some of kind of healing always occurs when we pray for it.

As He showed me so beautifully by healing my fingers at Mass, sometimes we are healed even when we do not ask for it. And we cannot forget that ultimately the most wonderful healing takes place when we breathe our last breath here on earth and are welcomed into our heavenly home. Jesus' victory over sin and death and the healing of the soul in which the body participates, are the most important and necessary healing, for the body will participate in the resurrection of the dead and share in the fruits of Jesus' sacrifice on the Cross. It is no wonder that His healing power is so intense in the Eucharist, which makes present the sacrifice of Calvary in an unbloody way. "By his passion and death on the cross Christ has given a new meaning to suffering: it can henceforth configure us to him and unites us with his redemptive Passion." (***CC, # 1505***)

This wonderful experience of the Lord Jesus powerfully validated what we believe as Catholic Christians — that *every* Mass is a healing Mass because the master Healer is truly present. However, I have learned over the years that the Lord often requires our cooperation in faith; being open to the possibility of divine healing makes healing more possible.

Perhaps most reassuring in reflecting gratefully on this particular blessing was the fact that the Lord took the initiative to heal me. I have come to believe that God often heals us of many illnesses and protects us from countless tragedies but we are unaware of them, so we assume that they do not happen. On the contrary, I think they happen all the time and I am learning to thank Him constantly for them, trusting in our Father's divine providence. The love of God is incredible and His healing power is available to all.

This experience also confirmed that we should always ask for physical and emotional healing before we automatically assume that every illness or trial is "God's Will" — that God wants us to suffer. That is because the essence of the gift of salvation is healing from the power of sin and death. All illness as we experience it is an effect of sin and eventually leads to death.

Jesus spent His entire life liberating the sick from their illnesses. He wholeheartedly accepted the inevitability of the Cross; He never asked for it. His death was the ultimate human act of evil. In fact, He begged our Father in the Garden of Gethsemane that if it be at all possible, the Cross be taken away. In the synoptic Gospels, even Jesus asked for a way out of suffering.

I believe that we need to follow His example in prayer — asking first for healing, especially after receiving Him in the Eucharist, and praying for the grace of acceptance if we recognize that the Lord seems to want us to join our suffering with His.

This healing and saving presence of God in His Son is available for us most powerfully during the Eucharist. It is worth any trouble, including turning our life inside out, to put daily Mass in the first place of our prayer life. It is worth getting up earlier, or juggling the day's activities, or even hiring a babysitter if the children are very young.

I believe that there is nothing in this life that should prevent us from coming daily or more often to the Lord's table if we are able to, because Jesus is really there simply for the asking, to be found in faith and obedience to His Word. He offers us salvation and eternal life, which every form of healing points to and participates in.

Let us not miss any opportunity to come together with our sisters and brothers in the Lord and receive the Lord Jesus, who can do infinitely more than we can ever ask or imagine if we only allow Him to in the gift of expectant faith (***Eph. 3:20***). Only He can strengthen us in every way to witness His love and bring the light of Christ to everyone in our world.

CHAPTER 9

*B*utterfly

For 'In him we live and move and have our being' . . .
(Acts 17:28)

I have always loved butterflies. When I was young, when
ever my family and I got out of the city for warm weather
day trips, I would delight in chasing butterflies. I
devised ways of sneaking up behind them when they were at
rest and catching them, putting them into jars with grass and
leaves and holes in the top, of course, so they could breathe.
(Don't ask how I learned that they needed bigger holes in the
top.) And when I had kept them long enough to admire their
beauty, I had sadly let them go.

Years later, when I was a busy young mother, butterflies
came into my life again, but this time the Lord used them to
teach me about seeing Him in the littlest things, and about His
limitless generosity.

We often ate at a local restaurant specializing in hamburgers.
The "penny a pound" specials were excellent so several moms in
the neighborhood would invariably pack up all the kids and take
them down for a lunch that could cost less than 50 cents per
child. After all, how much do little munchkins weigh?

One day, when the children were quite young, the Lord
gave us a lovely little gift in the restaurant parking lot. I was
getting everyone together as we were leaving our car, and it was
naturally a bit wild, since the children were anxious to get into
the restaurant to gobble up the free popcorn and beg to play
the games so enticingly set up around the room.

Just as we were preparing to start walking toward the restaurant, a beautiful, large yellow Monarch butterfly decided to come over and sit on my hand. It was totally surprising because I had stopped moving for only a brief moment, yet the butterfly found that one still moment.

When this lovely yellow visitor gently landed on my hand, we all stopped rushing and just looked at it as it moved its wings up and down. It was not in the least bit of a hurry to leave and I was not about to chase it away. We stood there and waited, not quite believing that this was happening, the children and I all with wide-eyed expressions of surprise and delight.

An ordinary day had been transformed. It is not often that butterflies stop to say hello to people. We had been forced to slow down and "smell the roses," and we all loved it. God our Father had taken an ordinary day and transformed it for us, and I have never forgotten it or the lesson it taught. There are moments of beauty that God provides for us all in our very ordinary days. We must be willing to stop and enjoy them, or they will pass us by and we will be the poorer for not having experienced them.

Recently, the Lord also gave me another "gift" and corresponding lesson involving butterflies. I wanted to take a photo of a butterfly, preferably a Monarch like the one we had seen so many years ago, possibly to use with this chapter. On a trip to the mountains I took a walk near our home there and came upon just the lovely creature I wanted to photograph.

A brilliant Monarch was perched atop a striking fuschia

thistle bloom. It was a single flower, sharply outlined and contrasted against a curtain of green foliage. What a great picture! And what a great picture I *missed!* I had left my camera down the 500 foot driveway and by the time I would have needed to retrieve it, the butterfly would have been long gone. In addition, I knew that the Monarchs would be migrating south soon, and there went my opportunity for a photo again for some time.

Rather than wasting time on finding a way to track down another butterfly, I surrendered my desire for a butterfly photo to the Lord and did not think about it again.

I have trusted Jesus to take care of things for me over the years time and time again, and seen Him work big and little wonders. He will always come through in a most generous way. I was not disappointed. He came through mightily and again I am so grateful.

On a November 1998 writing assignment to Monterrey, Mexico, for **The Catholic Spirit**, I found out where many of those Monarchs go for the winter. A good number of them spend the cold months in Mexico and they were there in Monterrey to meet me when I arrived.

The air was filled with so many butterflies of all different types that as I looked up into the air, it seemed as if we were covered by a blanket of butterflies. As high as the eye could see, they circled and drifted on the breeze, layer upon layer of little wings catching the wind and soaring effortlessly. At times it seemed as if it might as well have been snowing butterflies. I gasped the first time I saw them, not unlike my reaction to our "tame" butterfly of so many years ago.

Butterflies of black and gold, of blue and yellow and orange, filled the air within the city and far above it. When we traveled into the mountains one day above the cloud line up to the top of Chipinque, they were still with us *en masse*. And they were more than happy to pose for us. I got my picture and many more. And I even got to serve as one butterfly's chauffeur, a rather peaceful creature who used several of us as perches upon which to dry its wings before it could fly off again.

What an amazing experience! And I knew it was meant as a gift to me. I not only got my photo but the Lord provided in superabundance, which says a lot about what He is like Himself. He is the God of Life and generous superabundance, and the butterfly showers echo the prolific life and joy of which the Holy Spirit is the source. God can never be outdone in generosity.

I cannot help but think of all those pretty butterflies of my youth. How much effort it had taken to catch them, and when I had them I knew they were not mine. I knew that they were wild creatures and that I just could not keep them. I could not tame them or take their fear of me away. I could not live in their world. And so I tried to hold them just for a little while, in jars, always sad at letting them go.

The experiences I have shared were a "present" to us, a present to me. With no effort on my part, the butterflies had come to us. In the first story, a butterfly showed no fear and it lifted all of us out of our busy existence into a whole new world. For the first time in my life, a butterfly had let me in to its world and it was wonderful. And as for the butterfly showers of Monterrey, again I had been given the privilege of entering the world of butterflies. And of course, the Lord revealed more about Himself to me in both of those surprising meetings.

I have discovered over the years that God is very much like those butterflies, beginning with the symbolism of new life of the Resurrection of Jesus. For God so loved the world that He sent His only Son so that those who believe in Him might have life (*John 3:16*). He broke into our world permanently and set us free.

I have also come to see that the Lord breaks into our individual lives occasionally in powerful ways just to make sure we do not forget Him, because we get to running and moving so quickly that sometimes we might just need to get a very obvious wake-up call. I know that I have needed several of those.

It also seems to me that God provides touching and special moments throughout our lives all the time, but often we just do not stop to take the time to look at them. We write them off as coincidence or something nice, but never what they really are — little gifts from God, showing us that he remembers us, loves us, and wants us to notice Him in His creation, thus praying constantly as we admire the Author of such delicate encounters.

Perhaps sometimes we just try too hard. Sometimes we seem to think that we can take something beautiful for ourselves and hold tightly onto it, and then it is ours, as I tried to keep the butterflies of my youth. But it is not really ours until it gives itself to *us*. And that is something that can never be forced.

God's love is like that. He gives it so freely that we do not need to try too hard. We just need to be there in prayer, to tell Jesus we need Him and ask Him to come to us and He is there. He comes into our world and He does not go away. For He has humbled Himself and lived in our own world, and with His death and Resurrection, nothing will ever be the same. The power of darkness — the dominion of the evil one — has been broken. I've come to believe that we need not even believe in Him yet. We can call Him all the same in our doubt or despair or confusion, and beg Him to give us faith in Him, or increase our faith. He will answer.

I have also come to believe that in His infinite and very creative generosity, the Lord often likes to just provide delightful experiences for us, simply to see us smile. No amount of money could have bought these butterfly encounters. I have yet to meet a trainable butterfly.

The Lord can and does bless us with the most unique, incredible experiences because He is the Lord of all creation, and no one else is, but we need to pray and ask Him to open our eyes to see them. These graced encounters are the intangibles, the things that money and worldly power can never, ever buy. They are touches of pure love for God is Love.

May we all pray together for the openness to accept God's Love, and the courage and strength to follow Him wherever He wishes to take us, no matter what the cost.

CHAPTER 10

Calming the 'Savage Beast'

Peace I leave with you; my peace I give to you. Not as the world gives do I give it to you. Do not let your hearts be troubled or afraid.

(John 14:27)

When our oldest daughter Aileen had recently received Jesus in her First Communion, a touching episode in our home offered me the opportunity to point out Jesus' Real Presence in the Eucharist to my wide-eyed young daughter.

We have had every kind of little animal, be it guinea pigs and rabbits to white mice and bunnies, and at the time we were sharing our home with a rather nutty hamster. I cannot recall his name because there were just too many small pets who came to live with us for a short time. Their names have all become a big blur but I do remember this hamster's behavior. Holding onto him was almost an impossible task. This hamster did not know the meaning of the words "stay still," not even for a moment.

One evening after I returned from daily Mass, I had to hold onto Mr. Hamster for a few moments for Aileen. I prepared myself to move quickly as the little critter would undoubtedly try to dart out of my hands in every way he possibly could. I was surprised, however, by how he acted that night.

Rather than darting away as quickly as he could, the hamster snuggled up next to me and became completely calm. It was not as if he was asleep; on the contrary, he seemed wide awake, yet very peacefully resting cupped in my hands. It was unnecessary to try to hold him. He was not going anywhere.

Even Aileen, as young as she was, could not quite believe that her hyperactive little pet was behaving so differently than his characteristic perpetual motion. The Spirit prodded me to use this teachable moment.

What was different about this particular moment as opposed to any other moment in a busy day? I asked Aileen what she thought the answer might be, and then I answered it with the thought that came from the Holy Spirit and not myself.

What was different was the Eucharistic Presence of Jesus whom I had just received about 15 minutes previous to holding the hamster. The little guy could sense the Lord's Presence and it touched even him with total peace.

There was a poignant silence when Aileen and I both knew that what I had said was true. A sense of conviction, of the correctness of that observation, also known as the gift of discernment, was very clear.

The Presence of the Lord Jesus had calmed our little "savage beast." As the hamster rested peacefully, Aileen listened intently to a lesson on the Real Presence that was taught that night by the Lord through a hamster and interpreted by a mom.

A few minutes later, our tiny furball began to stir and the

calm gave way to the more usual storm. It was a chore just keeping him from dashing himself to the ground as he continued to try to escape.

But even now, when I recall the lesson the Lord taught us that day, I cannot help but wonder — just what can the Presence of the Lord do to calm our "savage beasts" if we give Him permission to do so?

CHAPTER 11

I Want My Mommy

But Zion said, "The LORD has forsaken me;
  my Lord has forgotten me."
Can a mother forget her infant,
  be without tenderness for the child of her womb?
Even should she forget,
   I will never forget you.
See, upon the palms of my hands I have written your name;
   your walls are ever before me.

(Isaiah 49:14-16)

There have been times when I've been sick as an adult that I almost wished that my "mommy" was still around to take care of me for a few days until I recovered. I understand that most people experience this kind of thing at one time or another in the face of illness. I suppose that is because there is nothing like a mommy to do things like tuck you in bed as a child and anticipate your needs before you can even think about them.

As adults, most of us "mommies" tough it out and stay sick longer than our children because we have to care for them. But that memory of how nice it once was to have your mother nurse you back to health never seems to disappear. And one night when I needed the special kind of care a "mommy" provided, the Lord took care of me in a gentle, wonderful way.

The winter is especially bad for sharing germs in a young family and as usual, I was fighting a virus which I had picked up along with the children. As I was putting the quilt over my daughter Aileen at bedtime, I felt so tired that I just wanted to drop. And I remembered with a sigh the days when I had my mommy to tuck me in the way that I was tucking in my daughter. Instead, I recall saying a quiet prayer inwardly asking for the Lord's healing and help, and uniting my illness with His suffering, the proverbial "offering it up" that has never lost its spiritual power. I swallowed my complaints, even to myself, which was not too easy considering the way I was feeling.

With the children down to bed, I was able to go into my bedroom and put my head down for a few minutes. Because the children were sick, I must have put them down to bed earlier than usual. It was early evening and was still fairly light outside, so this episode must have occurred either in the fall or the spring. It was too early for me to go to sleep, I thought, so without changing into a nightgown and getting ready for bed, I put my head down on the bed for what I expected to be a few short minutes, just to gain back some precious energy. In fact, I kept my glasses on because I anticipated being down for only about five minutes so I did not even climb under the covers, but stretched out on top of the quilted bedspread.

Once my head hit the pillow, however, I knew that I needed a real nap. I carefully placed my glasses on top of the bedspread on Steve's pillow next to me and was too tired to move. Still I anticipated only a few minutes rest. Instead, I woke up rather slowly in a dark room and realized that I must have been fast asleep for awhile. So much for a short nap.

Without even opening my eyes, I groggily groped for my glasses next to me and was immediately aware that I had not even moved from the position in which I had fallen asleep. The glasses were exactly where I had left them, but as I touched them I noticed that the surface beneath them was not the quilted bedspread but a smooth pillowcase instead. That was puzzling enough but when I opened my eyes and tried to move, I was completely startled to realize that I was *under* the covers, the bedspread was folded back perfectly (something that I never do) and the sheets were tucked in so neatly on all sides that I had difficulty turning over.

There was no way that I could have awakened, pulled down the spread and tucked myself in this way, with the sheets tightly tucked between the mattress and box spring completely around the bed. For the bed to be made up the way it was when I woke up, I would have to have been *in* the bed while someone tucked the covers in around me! Yet Steve had not been home when I put the children to bed, since at the time he worked in New York City and often got home well after they were already asleep. And he assured me later when I went back downstairs that he had not yet been upstairs at all that evening.

That night as I went back to sleep, still tired but very excited, I knew that the Lord had taken care of me in a way I cannot explain. I had not asked Him to do it; I could never have expected anything like this, and that made it all the more touching. I had not complained about not having help. I had just sighed my need, really to myself, and He had heard me and taken care of me. I was speechless because it was becoming increasingly clearer in my own heart that the Lord had tucked me in just like my "mommy" would have done for me when I was a child.

And that taught me more about Him. To our Father in heaven, we will always be little children, *His* little children, and because of Jesus He will always be our "Abba", our Daddy. I absolutely believe that it would not matter if no one on this planet loved or wanted us, although that is a terrible thing. *God* loves us. He is responsible for us. He has promised in His Word to take care of us if we entrust ourselves to Him. And the reality is that we always have people who love us in the Body of Christ.

Especially in this age of death as opposed to life, this realization has to be of great comfort and freedom. Not a single one of us is ever a "mistake". We make the mistake by rejecting the life that God has given, especially in abortion-on-demand, euthanasia, embryonic stem cell research and cloning, only some of the increasingly menacing ways that our societies find to cheapen human life.

Often we are blinded by sin and selfishness, and it is *we* who close the door to God, not He to us. Constant complaints block the Lord's ability to bless us, while not complaining opens the door to His always surprising grace. Time and time again, I have seen how just opening the door a tiny bit to the Lord is all that He needs to flood us with the graces and forgiveness we so desperately need. Like the Father in the parable of the Prodigal Son, our heavenly Father is waiting for us to come back to His love.

As usual, God's timing is a complete mystery. To expect Him to answer our every whim is childish because Jesus calls us to be child*like*, to trust Him completely and to acknowledge our need for Him, to be humble in His sight.

To expect Him to do something like what happened that night would have been, I believe, presumptuous at best. But *not* to expect the Lord to care for us as He chooses to, is to expect too little. In Heaven and in the deepest center of our being, where the Lord God waits for us with great patience, we always have a caring Father; a generous Savior, and a trusted and generous Friend and Advocate, who have given us a loving "Mother" — the special gift of our mother in faith, Mary. His love constantly covers us and wraps us up in Himself, just as He covered and cared for me that night. He is just waiting for permission to surprise us with His love.

CHAPTER 12

The Lord Provides

Bring the whole tithe
   into the storehouse,
That there may be food in my house,
   and try me in this, says the LORD of hosts:
Shall I not open for you the floodgates of heaven,
   to pour down blessing upon you without measure?
For your sake I will forbid the locust to destroy your crops;
And the vine in the field will not be barren,
   says the LORD of hosts. *(Malachi 3:10-11)*

*J*esus has been teaching me very patiently in many ways over the years that money is to be used for His purposes, and I am still learning this lesson. Two particular instances illustrated in a most graphic way that God will always provide for our needs if we seek His Kingdom first, and that He expects us to give some of our surplus to those in need.

Also, Jesus continues to show me that sometimes we are called to give more than we think we can, and that the Lord expects us to trust Him because He will provide for us through His people.

The first "lesson" involved the large sum of two dollars. My son Dan and daughter Mary Beth were involved in Honors Band while they were attending St. Augustine of Canterbury School. Although it was a great activity for the children, this "honor" meant that parents had to drive all over the state of New Jersey to frequent evening practices which ran late into the night. In order to lessen the stress on all of us, we formed carpools.

This particular night when it was my turn to drive, the practice was being held in a school in northern Jersey located just off the Garden State Parkway. In a confusing rush, I had placed my purse on top of the car in the driveway and inadvertently driven out with it perched on the top of my car. Fortunately, it dropped in the driveway but I didn't see it in the dark. I was off to band practice with no purse and I didn't even realize that it was missing.

My car had a change compartment which held just enough money this night to get me through the first few tolls on the parkway. As I approached the final toll booth, I asked the children in the back seat to hand me my purse because I did not have enough change to pay the toll. To my surprise, it was not there and I scrambled to put together enough cash, however small that amount was. The children did not have any money at all with them. I felt ridiculous asking for money from children, but it got worse than that.

I only needed 10 cents more to be able to pay the toll. I recalled that there was a dime stuffed under the driver's seat that I had left there for some time for no good reason. Now I was glad that I had listened to that little inner sense that had told me to leave it there. I scrambled to locate it and paid the toll with a sigh of relief. At least I had made it to my destination. As I pulled into the parking lot I thanked the Lord for getting me there. But now I had to get home and that dime had been the last of my cash.

I didn't know a soul at the practice except the instructor, whom I did not know very well at that point, but I realized that I would have to beg for a loan, however small, to be able to get home. Begging was not something I was used to doing. It made me quite uncomfortable, but a plea for one dollar from the instructor, the exact amount necessary for the trip back, yielded the loan. As ridiculous as it sounds, I felt so foolish having to ask for money. It didn't even feel as silly as having dropped my purse in the driveway. I believe that busy moms sometimes do dumb things and most often, thank the Lord, they are pretty benign. But to ask for money from a complete stranger, even just a dollar, *that* I found humiliating.

After attending evening Mass in the parish church, I knocked on the sacristy door and asked the celebrant if there was a phone I could use to call home and touch base with my husband about my missing purse. Somewhat reluctantly, the priest allowed me to use a phone in the sacristy and occasionally he appeared to look over at me with suspicion. I told my tale to Steve who promptly found the purse in the driveway and put my worst concerns to rest. I also told him how I had borrowed a dollar from the kids' music instructor and would be okay getting home. Still, I felt embarrassed.

I stayed to pray in the church for a few quiet moments after Mass, and noticed a different priest — probably a young associate in the parish — coming over to me. He sat down next to me, telling me that he had overheard my tale of woe in the sacristy (I had not even noticed him there) and that one

dollar certainly was not enough for me to travel with. He put
two dollars in my hand and insisted that I keep it. I insisted
that I pay him back but he asked only for prayers, to which I
agreed. I continue to pray for him although I have no idea who
he is. And I pray for the other priest too, because he seemed
so unhappy.

I was deeply touched by the gesture and spent some time
praying for this thoughtful man that night. It was only two
dollars but I felt like my immediate world was not such a cold
place any more. As I was getting ready to leave and spend
some time reading in the auditorium while the children practiced, it struck me that I was "rich" now. I had *three* whole
dollars and I only needed one dollar for tolls.

So I put one dollar into the poor box, keeping an extra
dollar just in case I needed it while bringing home my precious
young cargo. After all, I probably should have a little extra
change around all the time if possible. We made it home
just fine and I have *never* left my purse on the top of the car
again, although I have certainly done other absent-minded
things since.

I wish that in the third world, or in a poor slum here in our
own country, once could be enough for those who have to beg
constantly for food for that day, maybe even for that moment.
No one should have to beg for what is a right to life. Jesus
made it very clear that night that wishing and praying does not
do it. Perhaps our idea of what is "enough" is faulty. Especially here in the United States, it seems that we have inter-

changed what we "need" with what we "want". I learned that there is always a way to help someone else, even when I think I do not have *anything* to give. Pope John Paul II has repeatedly challenged the United States to renounce our materialism, and he is right in issuing such a challenge.

In a touchingly graphic way, Jesus illustrated that my trust was in Him, not in the money I needed. He showed in a simple lesson that when I did not have enough, He will not only provide enough but He will expect me to give some of it away. It is a matter of justice, a serious matter about which I will have to answer to the Lord at the end of my life. From my own humiliation, I knew that no one in the world should have to suffer the humiliation and mistrust associated with begging for the barest necessities when I am living in over-abundance.

When I placed that dollar bill in the poor box, the Holy Spirit inspired me to pray that, as the Lord Jesus had multiplied the loaves and fishes (*Mark 6:34-44; 8:1-9*) and as He so generously gives Himself to us in the Eucharist throughout the whole world day after day after day, that tiny dollar would be multiplied and do so much more than a mere dollar should be able to do. And I believe with all my heart that it was.

Even without divine intervention, a dollar can go a long way to relieve suffering in countries like Haiti and Guatemala. We have lived in the Caribbean and I have traveled to Central America to be with the poor twice, and I know first-hand how cruel life can be for them.

Sometimes I had thought before that evening that when we did not have a bigger amount to donate, it simply was not enough to give a very small amount. I recognized an embarrassment — really a form of pride — at not being able to give more, so sometimes I had not given the small amount and prevented the Lord's blessings in multiplying its yield. Despite the fact that I had seen so much suffering firsthand in the Caribbean, I still procrastinated at times and Jesus was gently showing me that I have much more to learn about trust.

Jesus teaches me that it is far better to give tiny amounts regularly than to wait to give that bigger donation, because that time may never come. Someone might die in the meantime, a tragedy that cannot be reversed and one for which I am at least partially responsible if I fail to respond to the Spirit's inspirations to share the wealth the Lord provides for me.

Since that day, the Holy Spirit prompts me to give whatever we have and always to ask that it be multiplied in expectant faith. I keep the dollar that I did not use for tolls in one of my

Liturgy of the Hours books and remember every time I see it
to thank God for all His blessings, and to ask Him to guide me
in responsibly tithing our money, time and talents so that His
Kingdom might come in its fullness.

A second "lesson" involved the amount of $100. The
children were still quite young, and Christmas was around the
corner. It certainly did not seem to be the time to be giving
away needed money, yet when a particular charity presented
itself both Steve and I were inwardly sure that the Lord Jesus
was telling us to give $100. And so we did.

That $100 was not extra cash. We knew that we would feel
its loss but it seemed so clear that we should give it away and
take the Lord at His word, trusting that He would take care of
us. We sensed that once we placed our trust in Him, we would
free Him to come up with some very creative solutions to our
financial needs.

Again the Lord used the situation to illustrate His creativity
and love for us. Very shortly afterwards, Steve received a check
in the mail as a Christmas gift for exactly $100 from someone
to whom he had given some professional advice. He had not
asked for payment but God had arranged through this man's
generosity that we get back the exact amount that we needed
to reimburse our donation. The Lord was teaching us how
to listen and confirming when we correctly heard and acted
on His voice.

At the risk of sounding very simplistic, I must say that the

Lord cannot be outdone in generosity. I keep learning daily that when we trust Him and try to listen to the Holy Spirit's inspirations, we become stronger and better able to follow Him when times are tough and His whispering voice must be discerned amidst countless distractions and difficulties, both good and bad.

It was good to know that we had heard His voice correctly, and that He had honored our gift by showing us that He does keep His promises, that He does hold us lovingly always. We did not ask for a sign but God provided it for us just the same. I am coming to see more and more that He is a touchable, lovable, caring and extremely interactive God who wants to be a part of our life. Jesus became one of us in the Incarnation, and offered us eternal life through His life, Death and Resurrection. The Lord wants us to always ask, to always seek, because in His own unique way, He always gives all of Himself to our requests. It is amazing and unfathomable how very much God loves us. There is nothing He would not do for each and every one of us.

The lesson the Lord taught me through both of these stories, and many other unnamed ones, is that our money is not ours. It, too, belongs to God who is Lord of all. He can provide two dollars or two million dollars. Power does not lie in money. Power lies in love, in God's love. No amount of money can buy the salvation of one human being and the life of one child who starved to death can never be purchased back.

We are called to care for one another on every level —

individually, in our parishes and communities, and around the world. Our money is meant to advance the Kingdom of God, to help bring about a world of justice and peace. We are challenged to help *all* people here on earth and to give glory to God alone in doing so. The Catholic Church has taken the call to justice and social action very seriously, and Pope John Paul II has developed that teaching first put forth in the modern age in Pope Leo XIII's encyclical ***Rerum Novarum*** in 1891. The inherent dignity of every human being is at stake, as is respect for every human life.

To respond to the Church's "option for the poor" we must ourselves realize how poor we are. Everything is the gift of a loving God. So if we love and trust Him, God will take care of us in surprising ways and use us in equally surprising ways to care for others. And He *always* keeps His promises.

CHAPTER 13

Roses In The Snow

As I wrote this chapter on the eve of the feast of St. Therese of the Child Jesus, I was delighted to recall several lovely experiences that confirmed for me that devotion to the saints is not pious nonsense, as some seem to think today. Rather, it is a constant teaching of the Catholic Church in the dogma of the Communion of Saints, and we assent to belief in that every time we say the Creed. The saints are our brothers and sisters in the Lord who have fought the good fight and triumphed, and who love us with a pure, powerful love — the undiluted love of God.

One day many years ago, when my children were still young, I decided to pray the novena to St. Therese for a special intention. I had heard that often the petitioner received roses upon completing the nine days of prayer, but I never felt it was necessary to ask for such a sign, and so I neither asked for nor expected a sign.

I had not even begun any formal prayers. In fact, I had just reached a decision to make the novena when my doorbell rang later that very same day. There on my front porch was one of my neighbors, the mother of two of my children's friends, and in her hand were a dozen magnificent red roses. She handed them to me. I was speechless. When I questioned why she had brought me roses she responded that she was compelled to bring them without really understanding exactly why; she was as puzzled as I was.

I continue to be amazed at this event after all of these years. And I was moved to realize that the young French nun who died about 100 years ago is not only a dear friend of the Lord but also our dear friend, and that He allows beautiful signs to cement that friendship, provided we do not get too hung up on signs and forget the God who gives them.

It seems as if dear Therese delights in sending roses as tokens of her love. I will never forget the cold, winter day when she gave me another charming assurance of her prayers.

One of two old rose bushes I planted many years ago in our backyard survived until just recently and every year, supplied me with many beautiful, red roses throughout the summer and often into the fall. But like most rose bushes it took a siesta for the winter, saving up its energy for the spring. Although I tried to cut it back in the fall, some years I never get to it and the long, sleeping stems were barren and looked quite dead throughout the winter. I believe that this particular winter I had not cut the bush back.

Once more I recall having thought of St. Therese and of my need of her prayers, and to my astonishment, the next day my barren, frozen, partially-snow-covered rose bush had two stunning, blood-red rose buds bursting into bloom, defying the icicles that touched their delicate petals. They had definitely not been there the day before.

Those surprising roses in the vase on my kitchen counter were for me not only a sign of eternal life, not only of the power of prayer, but also of the power of the intercession of the saints. A rose in the snow reminded me of Therese herself,

a beautiful sign of the love of God amidst a growing coldness and preoccupation with death in a world that continues to freeze our hearts, our consciences and our minds.

It seems to me that those who belittle devotion to the saints need to think again. Father Benedict Groeschel once mentioned in a class that it has to be the intercession of the saints in heaven that keeps the Church going here on earth, because we have made so much of a mess on our own that divine intervention and the prayer of the Church in heaven has to be what is sustaining us. I tend to agree with him.

To this day, almost every single time I turn to Therese, even before I can formulate a prayer, she anticipates my need and always somehow I find at least one rose showing up in my life, unexpectedly and always welcome, a link between us and a promise of a friendship that disarms me. Her love reveals the love of God for me. I know that she is much closer to me now than we ever could have been had I known her in her earthly life. And I look forward to meeting her in the Lord someday.

It is true that there are excessive pious practices that border on superstition. And there are simplistic and even theologically incorrect understandings of devotion to the saints. But that does not change the fact that the saints love us and are our friends in heaven. They are one with us, but now they gaze on the face of God and it is marvelous to have them bring us into the Lord's presence in prayer.

We don't hesitate to ask for prayer from our friends whom

we know are in a living relationship with God. It only follows
that those whom the Church has discerned are living with God
in heaven can certainly pray for us as well! The triumph of the
saints is the glory of God who redeemed them in Jesus just as
He redeemed us. By imitating them as they imitated Our Lord,
we hope to become saints ourselves. The Blessed Mother is
the greatest of the saints. It baffles me that anyone can object
to asking her to pray for us.

St. Therese is not the only saint with whom I feel very
close. Since I have been a young child, I have been very moved
by the stories of the lives of the saints, and regret that so many
young people today still seem to know so little about them.
The lives of the saints are a treasure for the Church, and I fully
believe that we need to bring them back as models for us all.

It is so comforting to know that we are not alone. Not
only do we have the Lord Jesus in His presence among His
people here on earth, in His Church, in His Word, in His
Sacraments and especially in His Eucharistic Presence where
He fully comes to us.

He is also present to us in the Communion of Saints, in
those who have gone before us. Their prayers for us are
priceless gifts provided to give us hope and courage that yes,
God will indeed complete the good work He has begun in each
and every one of us if we trust Him.

I can no longer look at a red rose without thinking of my
friend St. Therese. And I cannot look at a red rose without

thinking of the moving poem that weds the beauty of this delicate flower with the beauty of the Lord Jesus who died that we might be saved, that we might be part of the family known as the Communion of Saints. It doesn't seem to be accidental that red roses are so often St. Therese's special gift.

CHAPTER 14

Delaware Water Gap

On this mountain the LORD of hosts
    will provide for all peoples
A feast of rich food and choice wines,
    juicy, rich food and pure, choice wines.
On this mountain he will destroy
    the veil that veils all peoples,
The web that is woven over all nations;
    he will destroy death forever.
The Lord GOD will wipe away
    the tears from all faces;
The reproach of his people he will remove
    from the whole earth; for the LORD has spoken.

(Isaiah 25: 6-10)

I have come to see that certain things in life happen to us especially to teach us how God sees things. They show us how differently He views our lives from how we view them when we try to function without surrendering to His vision for our lives.

For me, one of these "things" happens to be tied to a special location. For some reason, many years ago when I drove through the Delaware Water Gap on U.S. Route 80 between New Jersey and Pennsylvania for the very first time, I fell in love with this beautiful place.

I have been blessed to witness so much natural beauty in

my life — so many wondrous places — and yet my favorite still remains the Delaware Water Gap. I've seen views from the top of the Shenandoah Mountains in Virginia; the mountainsides and valleys in Haiti dotted with farms like verdant patchwork quilts, and the rolling hills and winter sunsets in the English countryside outside London. I've been privileged to drive through the mountains near Denver being blanketed by snow as buffalo roamed near ghost towns; to stand on a mountain-top above the clouds surrounding Monterrey, Mexico, and to swim, sail and snorkel in the blue-green waters of Guantanamo Bay, Cuba, reflecting the mountains and white sand beaches that encircle it.

Yet my heart still soars every time I have to drive through the Delaware Water Gap. I know it has something to do with the power and majesty of nature that is so exquisitely apparent in the exposed sedimentary rock faces, a photograph of power so immense that it folded and crumpled these solid walls like tissue paper. I know that it has something to do with the balanced angles and curves of the Delaware as it weaves its way through the gorge it carved out over the course of hundreds of thousands of years. It is a humbling experience to drive through the Delaware Water Gap. The rock faces tell of a history that places our own short lives in proper perspective. It always makes me feel very small to drive through the gap because I am very small, as we all are. That is not frightening to me; rather, it situates me squarely in the heart of God the Father, who has promised to care for His fragile children because we are so very small in the universal view of things.

And I know that I'm not alone in my attraction to this place, since it is always abounding with tourists and hikers, young and old, who also come back again and again to see the river change moods, or to watch the leaves glowing in shades of crimson and gold, or to float down the current of the lazy summer waters.

When I encounter the Water Gap, I encounter my Father in heaven in a special way every time. It is as if the entire scene was painted for me, and in a sense, that is true. The Father has placed me in this tiny moment in time to enjoy Him in His magnificent creation, as He has done for each of us in our own little places. In every rock, every tree, every glistening drop of water, God my Father whispers, "I love you," through the Delaware Water Gap. It is always a gift for me.

When we built a vacation home in the Pocono Mountains of Pennsylvania, I was obviously delighted that I would be passing through my favorite place so often. We built it with the express purpose of sharing it with others as a place to spend some quiet time with the Lord. Little did we know all that would transpire over the years that we traveled between New Jersey and Pennsylvania.

Shortly after barely finishing the house-building project, I was struck with the serious cancer that almost claimed my life. Steve's consulting contract was ended and he could not locate any work for nearly a year. It was as if a black cloud fell over us and we lived in total darkness, trusting solely in the Lord, living in faith as a couple as we never had before.

Yet in all that time of sharing in the Lord's suffering, every single time that we drove through the Water Gap my heart still sang. Nothing could take that joy away. I was reminded that I am loved by a faithful Father and I could not be anxious. Even if for only a brief moment, my every concern seemed to disappear when we entered into the Gap, which extends a few miles on the New Jersey side before reaching the Delaware River. I still heard the Lord's whispers to me, but now He was saying, "I love you. Trust me."

Things have stabilized a great deal after that initial time of incredible darkness, and I believe that we have grown a great deal in our love for one another in our family, and in the love of the God who so gently held us in the palm of His hand throughout that time. And so now the trip through the Delaware Water Gap has also become a symbol for me of the rock-solid love and faithfulness of God the Father for His children. And naturally I love it even more.

I truly believe that, in a way that I would never have asked for or imagined, the Father gave us a special gift by inspiring us to build a home in Pennsylvania, a home that became a financial burden almost instantly due to so many unforeseen and overwhelming circumstances beyond our control. One of those was the bottom falling out of the real estate market in that area, making it impossible for us to sell the property because we would lose a great deal of money. Yet, although it may seem inside-out, I am beginning to see that God's view of our world makes our world-view look inside-out, simply because it is.

The joy I experienced each and every time I drove through

the Gap only confirmed more deeply that the Lord does not seem to see a huge financial burden to be a problem at all. It brought us to trust Him implicitly and therefore became a blessing. Even more incredible than that, He knows how much I love the Gap, and renting our home forced us to drive there often for some time. Each time we passed through I said a special prayer of thanksgiving. I truly believe that it's possible for this prayer alone to have been worth far more to our Father in heaven than all of the problems building and owning the home presented to us.

What I have come to see is that the Lord is not about having everything so neat and tidy that we have no need to trust Him; I've come to see that He values trust so highly that He allows situations to occur not only to build up our faith, trust and love of Him, but also to gift us with what He sees as the more important matter at hand. And in my case, it was bringing me into His presence in a special way every time I drove through this wonderful part of His creation. He quite simply put us there to bless us. When the time was right, a perfect young couple bought our home in December 2000. In retrospect, our losses don't seem to be very great in comparison to the graces with which we were blessed for those 11 or so years. And each drive through the Delaware Water Gap will always be a blessing.

My prayer is that all of us learn how to "see" with God's eyes because if we can, then nothing is a burden, nor is it too difficult or unexpected or confusing. If God is at the heart of them, then all of life's blessings and burdens are sources of grace.

CHAPTER 15

Lemonade and Motor Oil

There is an amazingly playful side to our God, a God whose Holy Spirit hovered above the waters and whose Wisdom "played" before Him as the world was created (***Proverbs 8:30-31***). Jesus came that we might have joy in its fullness (***Jn. 15:11***), and to be filled with joy presumes a sense of humor. But it seems to me that more often than not, one of the ways that we can keep Jesus at a distance is that we think He doesn't have a sense of humor. We forget that through His Son, God the Father created the gift of laughter in the first place!

For my husband Steve and me, the Lord's sense of humor has been revealed in several wonderful ways over the years, but the two examples that follow made lasting impressions in the lessons I believe they were meant to "impress" upon us.

The first occurred when I was going through an intensely difficult time in my spiritual life — several months during which my prayer was simply "hanging on," trusting that the Lord would make everything clear to me in His own way and in His own time. I was ready to wait, but the wait was a painful one and had already extended over a period of about six months.

At the time, I kept a little bookmark with an uplifting message hanging on my key holder in the kitchen, and I looked over at it countless times because it made me laugh and gave me hope. I still keep it in my day planner. It states, "When life gives you lemons, make lemonade," and the illustration showed some silly-looking lemons with smiles on their lemon faces sitting next to — you guessed it — a glass of lemonade.

Rather than dwell on my difficulties, I would say a prayer each time I looked at that bookmark. I would tell Jesus that I trusted Him, and that I believed in Him and in His love for me. It didn't lessen the heartache or immediately answer my questions, but it did lift my spirits and comforted me in a lighthearted way. Jesus used those little prayers to teach me something new about Himself. He dispelled all my doubts and healed my aching heart through His own sense of humor, and I fell in love with it.

This particular evening I was attending what has come to be known as a Healing Mass, a Mass where the charismatic gift of healing and the other gifts associated with the healing ministry are encouraged and included during the celebration of the Eucharist. (In reality, *every* Mass is a Healing Mass, for we receive the Master healer in Eucharist — see Chapter Eight.) I expected the Lord to "speak" to me in some way, to reveal Himself to me somehow, but never in the way that He did.

After receiving Jesus in the Eucharist, the group of about 25 people formed a circle and held hands, asking the Holy Spirit to be active among us as we adored the Lord Jesus completely present with us. It was a very solemn time, a time of union with Jesus and with each other.

A woman began to speak about a "picture" the Lord was showing her in her mind, a vision or "word of knowledge" He was revealing to her. Admitting that she did not understand what it was that the Lord was showing her, she continued anyway. Obviously puzzled, she described seeing a tall, frosty glass and then seeing something quite unlikely — lemons! At this point, I opened my eyes as a smile began to creep over my face. She hesitated because it truly seemed ridiculous when she began to describe the process of making lemonade. I was so filled with joy that I told the surprised group out loud what it meant — when life gives you lemons, make lemonade! And all doubt and concern washed away from my mind and my heart in the space of a heartbeat.

Do you believe it? Our all-powerful, all-holy God whose only Son gave His very life for us, who has been adored through endless ages by myriads of angels and saints, has a great sense of humor! As a good Father, He knew that laughter was the best medicine. Inwardly, I regained strength and knew that I was pursuing the right course at the time.

Another amusing incident stands out in my mind. Early on in our faith walk as a couple, the Lord taught Steve and me very clearly that no matter what, if we need help, pray first! We still laugh about this one.

While Steve drove home late one evening from northern New Jersey many years ago on the New Jersey Turnpike, our rotary-engine station wagon decided to die in the left lane of traffic, forcing him to pull the car over on the center island during rush hour traffic, a feat in itself. A quick inspection led him to an awful discovery: there was not a single drop of oil in the engine.

One needs to understand the then "new" rotary engine to understand how something like this could happen. Let it suffice to say that this car burned up quarts of oil very rapidly. Unless it was constantly monitored, the oil level could drop drastically in as little as a week, and it was probably just a simple oversight with some complicated consequences.

With flashers blinking, Steve stood as cars and trucks whizzed by him at Indy 500 speeds, with no one attempting to stop and help him. In those days of pre-cellular phones, I began to wonder where he was when the clock showed that he was an hour and a half later than his usual arrival time at home. Meanwhile, out on the turnpike, Steve was getting concerned because not a single state trooper had passed him by and it was now getting dark, with rush hour traffic ebbing, reducing whatever chances there were that a good Samaritan might lend a hand. Close to three long hours went by and Steve was just about ready to give up when he realized that he had not said a prayer. So he did. And what happened after that is most amazing and amusing.

Almost immediately, a pickup truck came to a quick stop in front of him. The driver was an auto mechanic. Although his truck was a private vehicle, it was well-equipped with various auto parts including, of course, five very necessary quarts of motor oil. It turned out that the mechanic could relate very well to Steve's situation. He explained to Steve that he, too, had once been stranded when his truck also completely ran out of oil and ever since then, he has made it a point to always carry oil and other basic auto supplies, "Just in case someone else might need it." What on earth are the odds of *that*, on the New Jersey Turnpike no less?

With five fresh quarts of oil in the car, Steve took the man's name and address and when he got home very late to a very relieved family, we immediately dropped a check off to our highway "angel" for the cost of the oil. Steve emphasized that the stranger had arrived immediately after his prayer, and we both commented that he should have prayed first as we had a good laugh together.

Although very different, these two examples of how the Lord revealed His humorous side have a common thread running through them — that God's sense of humor is as real and as loving and as healing as any of the more "serious" gifts we receive from Him.

God is Love, so then love, as defined by St. Paul in *1 Cor. 13:4-13*, is the essence of His sense of humor. Divine humor never hurts. It is affectionate, gentle, respectful and uplifting. The Lord's sense of humor is holy, patient and kind. It does not mock people, or make off-color comments and is most certainly not crude. It is not what the world considers to be humor.

Because it is a conversation with Him, it is prayer; it is a touch of the Lord that is filled with the playfulness of the Holy Spirit, the Spirit of joy. Yet as prayer, it always has a solemn character to it, making it completely appropriate during a time of meditation after Communion in a celebration of the

Eucharist.

St. Teresa of Avila understood this aspect of God's character, and she quipped back to Him as easily as she bowed before "His Majesty," which is a term she most fondly and frequently used to address Our Lord. Throughout her many writings, but especially in her **Life**, Teresa seems to speak rather familiarly to Jesus, and her words are charming and probably quite disarming to the Lord. It seems that she shared the Lord's sense of humor and found it another way to enjoy Him and His presence, while never being disrespectful in any way.

Jesus tells us simply, "Come to me, all you who labor and are burdened, and I will give you rest." (**Matt. 11:28**) In my own experience, He makes it possible for me to laugh at my difficulties, if even for a brief moment, confirming that He is indeed there and with His help, I will make it through anything that comes my way, and for that matter, come out stronger for it. For me, Jesus without a smile is an incomplete God.

Friends are like that. I have never had a friend with whom I could not share a good laugh.

Jesus no longer calls us slaves; he calls us friends (**John 15:15**). I have learned and continue to learn that when we open ourselves to a real friendship with Him, I have seen amazing paths open up before me, things that were always there but that I could not see because of the blinders of self-absorption. Perhaps we are afraid to laugh with the Lord because we are afraid that He will laugh *at* us instead of with us, or perhaps we

are afraid that if we discover for ourselves just how real He is, He might ask us to change our lives.

Undoubtedly He will. He will ask us to trade our sadness brought on by sin for the joy of His friendship, and save us from the misery of sin and death. He will give us a gift of joy that the world can never give (*Jn. 14:27*). He will abide in us through the power of the Holy Spirit (*Jn. 14:17*), and His Holy Spirit will guide us to all truth (*Jn. 16:13*).

And if we give Him permission, He will be our dearest and most loving Friend, sharing the love of God the Father with whom we can share our deepest selves, unafraid to delight in Him as He does in us.

CHAPTER 16

Consider

the Lilies

The Lord is the best teacher I know, a teacher who tenderly confirms and goes out of His way to let us know that we have learned our lessons well. The following two examples taught me always to focus on life and never on death, and that trusting God and following His inspiration always "bears fruit" for others and ourselves.

Whenever I heard the passage of *Matthew 6:26-27* describing how God the Father cares for the lilies of the field and the birds of the air, I was touched by His gentle care. Yet even as a child, the thought would sometimes slip into my mind that birds don't live forever. I couldn't help but wonder about the birds that died.

On a street near my home that is heavily traveled, I have seen many a bird who was not as fast as the car it darted in front of. One day while driving home along that very street, a bird flew directly in front of the wheels of my car, narrowly missing being clipped by my car. And of course I thought about the dead birds.

The Lord chose this moment to teach me more about seeing things through His eyes, about trusting in Him and in His providence, rather than giving in to the discouragement and cynicism that so pervades today's society. With a light to my mind, the Lord Jesus whispered the words inwardly to me, "Don't look at the *dead* birds, Carolyn."

And all at once, I realized that to focus on the "dead birds," or the negative in anything, was not what faith in Jesus is all about. In a split second, I understood in a deeper way all that I had been taught about Christian salvation, all that I had believed because the Word of God said it and the Church taught it. I knew intuitively with a wonderful, hope-filled joy that God the Father does indeed care for our every need, no matter how absurd it might look, because He will turn all of our crosses into a share in Jesus' Resurrection. It was a moment of grace.

The Fathers of Vatican Council II accurately painted a picture of the times when they wrote about the modern world. In *Gaudium et Spes* (*The Church in the Modern World*), they described a world of rapidly changing social orders that is hopeful and yet anguished, striving to answer deeper questions of meaning and at the same time, imbalanced. "In the midst of it all stands man, at once the author and the victim of mutual distrust, animosity, conflict and woe." (*GS, # 8*)

The Council Fathers observe that fallen human nature is hopeless without the salvation that Jesus offers. Melancholy, even despair, pervades our existence. Our disdain for religious faith pervades some of the laws of our countries. It is hard to live on this planet and not to pick up some of that lack of respect for life and the hopelessness that causes it.

In an instant Jesus changed me and my way of thinking. He dispelled some of the darkness of my mind and opened my eyes to expectant faith in a deeper way, using the example of some of his tiniest creatures — birds — as He had for the His people 2,000 years ago. I had been looking at the *wrong* birds and realized in a new way that it is completely in my power with

God's grace to shift my focus consciously to life. In fact, I learned in that graced moment that it is absolutely essential to shift our focus to life, or forces around us will overcome us and we will "absorb" our "culture of death," as Pope John Paul II has so often called the anti-life attitudes that have gained a foothold in the United States and in the so-called "civilized" world.

I have also come to see that sometimes the Lord chooses to show us what He is doing through the inspiration of the Holy Spirit even when we do not ask Him, even when we have no need to know. The following example edified and strengthened the faith of many people, which is why I believe the Lord allows these little touches of light to happen — that we might witness to Him with greater conviction.

When the children were young I used to arrange for a babysitter to watch them while I went to daily Mass. I could not and cannot live without our Eucharistic Jesus daily, and need the fellowship of those who gather at the Lord's table with me daily as the Body of Christ. It was easiest for me to go to an early evening Mass at the nearby Consolata mission center.

Unable to attend Mass one day because I was sick with a virus, I was inspired in prayer during the day to offer my suffering as a prayer for all those who had cancer. Without question, I was confident that God would use my prayers as He saw fit; I had no need to know for whom I was praying. Above all, I offered the Lord Jesus my desire to receive His Precious Body and Blood because my inability to do so was much more difficult for me than being sick.

As I rested on the couch in the living room that afternoon, the doorbell rang and I was surprised to see a priest friend from the mission center, Father Renato Saudelli, standing there when I opened the door. He seemed puzzled, but stated simply that he had just come from bringing Communion to a man dying of cancer in the nursing home, and had an extra consecrated Host and felt compelled to stop here. "Do you want to receive Jesus in Communion?" he asked me.

Completely surprised, I enthusiastically said yes, explaining my sickness, my prayer for cancer victims and my overwhelming desire to attend Mass. Both he and I praised the Lord Jesus who had responded to my need to receive Him in such an incredible way, confirmed the prayers I had offered all day, and united me with one of the people for whom I had been praying.

Sometime later that evening, as Father Renato celebrated the Mass I would have attended had I been well that night, he shared joyfully with the congregation the story of how responding to the Holy Spirit's inspirations had brought us all together. The Lord Jesus had shown us how intimately He is always at work in His people, inspiring us and making us one with Him and each other in our sufferings and our joys, all united as His Body in Eucharist by the power of the Holy Spirit.

I am grateful to God for this experience that delighted me and increased my trust that every least little sigh of our hearts is heard by the Lord, and answered in perfectly marvelous ways that are lovingly personal and meaningful. For although some-times we do not know why we pray, or for whom we are praying, or why difficult and confusing things happen to us and prayers sometimes seem to be unanswered — in other words, if we are tempted to look at the "dead birds" — the Lord will reveal Himself to us in His own way, often anticipating our need, *if we trust Him.*

And we can also be sure that in addition to the Lord and the saints in heaven, someone is *always* praying for us, for the Holy Spirit inspires the members of the Body of Christ here on earth in incredible and mysterious ways to support one another.

CHAPTER 17

Lessons In The

Darkness

For though the fig tree blossom not
        nor fruit be on the vines,
Though the yield of the olive fail
        and the terraces produce no nourishment,
Though the flocks disappear from the fold
        and there be no herd in the stalls,
Yet I will rejoice in the LORD
        and exult in my saving God.
GOD, my Lord, is my strength;
        he makes my feet swift as those of hinds
        and enables me to go upon the heights.
                        (Habbakuk 3:17-19)

It was just a very little prayer, almost a whisper. It came from very deep within me, as if it were placed there by the Holy Spirit and I was simply responding to the inspiration. I am sure it was. It was like a sigh — a desire to know the Lord better. But when I said it and meant it, I knew that a change had already begun in me. Little did I know the impact that my small prayer would have on what seemed to be the stability of my life.

Almost instantly, perhaps the day after I uttered that prayer, it was as if the light completely went out spiritually and I was left in a deep spiritual "darkness" from around November 1975, after the birth of our second child, my son Daniel, until at least June 1976. It was a piercing kind of darkness where all sense of the Lord's Presence disappeared — completely. The Lord, my love, was gone, or so it seemed.

Dan had croup often and was difficult to put down to sleep at night. I had to walk with him for an hour every evening before he would finally fall asleep. Aileen, his four-year-old sister, was going through a bad time and hardly slept at night herself. I felt like a zombie.

To complicate things, I was ill constantly that winter. I caught one bad flu and then another very serious one right behind it. I was exhausted and it was a Catch-22 situation; I got sick because I was sick and nothing was breaking the cycle. I finally ended up catching a virulent flu that was going around that winter of 1976 and almost ended up in the hospital. My fever spiked to 105 degrees in about an hour, and Steve had to give me an alcohol rub to break it and bring it down to 103 degrees. I was so weak I could not even walk and my ears were ringing so loudly that I couldn't hear very well. And I had to temporarily stop nursing the baby.

I am sure that all of this sounds very familiar to new moms and moms of young children. But God used it all as part of an experience that spiritual writers, especially Carmelite St. John of the Cross, call a "dark night," a time of purification and great blessing because it truly heals and frees us in ways that nothing but deep suffering can do. The problem was that I knew nothing about things called "dark nights" at the time. Even knowing that such things happen might have been a help.

But the Lord got me through. The description that follows,

and appears throughout this chapter, will include some selections from my journal entries written in 1984. I chose to use it because it was written much closer to the actual experience.

All my sense of God's loving Presence was gone, totally gone. All my life, all I had had to do was think of Jesus and He was with me. He had drawn me into prayer so many times. I had failed Him . . . so often, but I had loved Him and grown to be so comfortable with this God who seemed always to be there for me, one way or another.

But now everything was different. It was worse than being abandoned. It was as if I couldn't even remember having known God's love ever in my life, and yet believing despite all else that it must have been that way. It almost seemed as if it had been someone else's experience, not my own. I dreaded the mornings. I longed to go to sleep at night so I could escape the days, although even at night I often didn't get any rest. I even reached the point where I didn't want to go on living. I was so tired in every way that I almost wanted to die. It was easier than facing a life that seemed to have dried up.

. . . I needed so much to get to Mass and Communion, and I was so sick and so tired that I couldn't go. I remember just plugging along, believing it had to get better. My prayer life was different. I couldn't pray. All I could do was fight like crazy all the thoughts and suggestions that seemed to be attacking me on all levels.

Horrid temptations were assaulting me all the time —
thoughts like "God never existed; you were a fool to have
believed in Him," and "There is nothing else." These thoughts
seemed to make perfect sense. I felt like I really was dying inside
and the Lord who had always been there for me, with His sweet
greetings and tenderness and love, was nowhere to be found.

There were a few "signs" that God was doing something
during my ordeal, even though I had no clue what that was.
One night I was awakened during the middle of the night to a
living nightmare. And I was not dreaming, as I believe I had
not been the night that the devil had frightened me as a baby in
my room.

I opened my eyes to "see" the bedroom bathed in an eerie,
reddish light that I can best describe as being a "dark" light.
The walls appeared to be coming in on me, and our bed
seemed to be rising off the ground. I was shocked, frightened
and didn't believe this was actually happening, but I knew that I
wasn't dreaming. I looked quickly over to my left at Steve
sleeping peacefully next to me and remember being amazed
that he was sleeping through all this. In fact, it was that glance
at my husband that I remember anchored me and helped me to
realize that this was a spiritual event. I turned to my right
slowly because I heard a hideous laugh.

It was a laugh like I had never heard before. It was deep
and cruel, a perfect match to the creature from which it issued.
Something evil was "standing" within a foot of me, next to my
bed, laughing triumphantly. No words were spoken but I felt

myself attacked in my mind with every insult. "He can't save you," the devil was somehow telling me inwardly about the Lord. "I have you now and He cannot help you." I was being horribly tempted to believe that I was lost.

Fear gripped my heart, but by the grace of God I recognized it and its source. I said one word, "Jesus", and everything disappeared instantly as I sat there in stunned awe. It had all happened so fast. I was aware of this Jesus in a deeply powerful way, but I did not "feel" a thing. I was truly awed by the power of Jesus' name. A soft peace came over the room and I fell asleep, exhausted and amazed.

> . . . I was constantly being tempted to give up on God through this whole time, which really . . . lasted until at least June. Once the devil was even allowed to suggest audibly (inwardly) to me that if I were to "call" him, he would take away all my sickness because he had the power to do it, and was being given power over me. And then he showed me a picture in my mind of just how, just what the first step would be, for me to "call" him. I felt like I was on the edge of a cliff. I felt almost as if I was already lost, in his clutches. But there was that spark of something deep within me that fought back. I was living my faith now. There wasn't a feeling to be found. I never even responded to the devil's suggestions. I continued to live as if he had never made them. But even these things only made me more certain that despite all the appearances, God had to exist or there wouldn't be a devil! Yet it's an impossible thing to describe . . . (The devil) would

*often taunt me with, "Where is your God now?" I ignored
him. It had to have been grace. Someone was definitely praying
for me. I know one Person who was doing a lot of praying
for me.*

*One night I was awakened again, and I was facing left again
as I awoke. But this time I was instantly awake and the
Presence I sensed in the room was powerful, but so peaceful.
The room was light, a soft white light. And I raised myself
up to see its source. The source of light was a Person. He
was absolutely beautiful, not so much because of His features,
but because of that soft, alive light that was literally
penetrating Him and diffusing through the whole room. He
was kneeling at the side of my bed, near Steve's armoire,
with His hands to His sides but slightly raised with the
palms up, I believe, because I couldn't see His hands . . .
(The man's) eyes were closed and He was in prayer. He
seemed to be very intense in His prayer. He was wearing a
simple while tunic, and His hair was shining like gold, but
somehow I knew that it was dark. It was that light, that alive
light, that literally made it shine like gold!*

*The peace I experienced was so incredible that it seemed to
me that this Person's Presence was the most normal,
comfortable thing in the world. God was with me. It was
the way it should be. That's how it seemed at the time.
Every thought, worry and care disappeared. The first thought
I had was that this Person sure looked like Jesus as I would*

picture Him to look, but this man looked more Jewish. I remember thinking that the Sisters (in grammar school) had said that visions didn't happen much any more, or something to that effect, and I actually felt so comfortable and peaceful that I turned over and went back to sleep! I slept more peacefully than I'd slept in months. I probably hadn't slept in months. And it wasn't until I woke in the morning that I realized that I had experienced Jesus in my room, praying, and now I can see that He was praying for me — I certainly needed it — and I hadn't even consciously recognized Him . . . Jesus' glorified Body is a definitely different experience. I can understand the Gospels and how people didn't recognize Him, not just once but several times. There is something very different about His life now in His glorified Body that literally cannot be recognized by us in this life unless God graces us to be able to do it. As I awoke that morning I knew it had been Jesus, and I was filled with such a deep peace. As time went on, I only became more inwardly convinced that it had been the Lord.

I drew from the effects of Jesus' prayer for me during the rest of my darkness, because after this experience, I went back almost immediately into the gloom I'd been living in. It almost seemed as if that moment hadn't happened. It almost seemed by contrast to make the darkness even darker by virtue of its light. Yet I knew deep within me that Jesus had come and I was awed by His Presence which I couldn't "feel" as I used to, but which I believed and knew in a deeper, "strange" way. I realize now that I was like an onion that had been peeled, layer by layer, until all that remained was the center. And now God was working in there.

I remember getting to Mass on Pentecost Sunday that year. I was so excited just to get there! I was also so weak. I remember the weakness. My knees felt like jello. But I received such a deep insight into the Holy Spirit at that Mass, and I was allowed to recognize Him in all the many events of significance in my life that I was able to say, "It was You! It was You all the time!" It was like meeting the real Wizard of Oz behind the curtain but not being disappointed!

During this darkness . . . all my self-pity came right to the surface. I saw so much ugliness in me that I hated it. I knew I didn't want that to be in me at the same time and I tried, but I fell a lot. By the time of Pentecost, I was starting to gain back some strength on all levels. I remember going to Danny's room one day and literally yelling at Jesus, "What are you doing to me?" But even that question implies that I knew somewhere in me that He was doing something. Even in the middle of that mess the deepest part of my heart knew that. Of course, I didn't get an answer verbally, but in a sense my answer was already in my heart and I knew it . . .

One day I sat down in Danny's room again, and went directly to Jesus who was in my heart but could have been light years

away for how I knew that, and told Him out loud, "I don't know what You're doing, but I know You still exist and I still love You." From that moment on, something changed. It was over. I was going to "make it."

Rather than having everything restored all at once, I gradually experienced more "light" coming back daily. I even started to recover from my illnesses, and so did Dan. No longer did it seem like the enemy was able to constantly torture me inwardly. I could think again and I could pray. They were definitely the prayers of a weak warrior, but they were there. And it was during this time that I realized that when I had been unable to pray, it was Jesus Himself praying for me, as He had in my room that night.

I felt inside as if I was still in darkness, like a diver coming up to the surface from a very great depth where the water was pitch black. But I was rising and I could feel it. All was black around me, but I knew that sensation of rising and I knew it would get brighter and I would reach the surface eventually. This time lasted about a month. All was peace. There was no more oppression. God was with me in a part of me that was too profound for me to understand. He still is. I recognized this to be that spark within me that had kept me from falling over the cliff during the past few months.

. . . I looked carefully at myself during this time, especially at my selfishness, and I decided I would never be that way

again. But now it seemed possible for me to make such a decision and hope to follow through in some way because I saw everything differently. It was as if blinders had fallen off my eyes and I hadn't even known they had been there in the first place. I was a different person, radically different from the person I had been even a few months before. I was so ashamed of my resentment and my selfishness. Jesus was yet to work even more on my pride, and He always continues to do so.

*What was so amazing was that life was just going on as usual to those around me. All they saw was a young crabby mother of 28 who was sick all the time and had had a "bad winter" with the kids. Aileen even ended up with double pneumonia in June that year. I had her fourth birthday party that March and did laundry and was probably an awful grouch while I was going through this period. It was all so ordinary. And God used it to give me His Life more abundantly, to draw me into union with Himself. I do believe with Father Benedict Groeschel (in his book **Spiritual Passages**) that most "dark nights" happen at office desks and kitchen tables (pg. 132). We just haven't bothered looking there very much . . .*

Hope grew stronger as the light grew brighter, as if I were a diver beginning to see light, then being gradually bathed more and more in the light of the warm, jewel-like tropical waters through which I was ascending, and being able, at long last, to see the surface above me, glittering and bright. There is nothing to describe how beautiful the surface of tropical water looks when you have gone down to 10 feet or so to harvest a sea fan and you have been down awhile, so your lungs are screaming for air. I know that the analogy is so perfect because I snorkeled in Guantanamo Bay in the early 1970s when Steve was stationed there with the U.S. Navy.

The day I "broke through the surface" is etched forever in my memory. It came in the form of a phone call from my friend, aptly named Mary, who lived in Norfolk, Va., at the time. Mary and Jim had been Navy friends of ours while we were stationed in Athens, Ga., and we had kept in touch for a while after Steve's four years of service were up.

Mary proceeded to tell me that while she had been praying, the Lord revealed to her that I had been very sick and that she should call me. I was astonished because she was right, and then she began to tell me about how she had been attending prayer meetings in Virginia where the gifts of the Holy Spirit were breaking forth in something called the Catholic charismatic renewal. I felt the Spirit's inspiration and knew why everything had happened as it had, all at once in a swift insight. And it was suddenly very clear that there had been one thing (that I was aware of) that I had been too afraid to surrender completely to the Lord all these years. The best way to describe it was that I could not and did not say a definitive "no" to the Lord in this area, but I couldn't say a definitive "yes". I had been praying for that grace of surrender for many, many years. Surprising even myself, I told Mary why I had been sick

— that I believed that it had been a "test" from the Lord. To both God and her, I declared out loud that it was time to stop saying "no" to Him and trust Him totally in this one particular fear. And joy burst out within me and over me so suddenly and powerfully that I thought I would die of joy right there on the phone!

> *. . . It was as if I was flooded from head to toe with power and my heart was literally burning with Love, with the Love I'd known all my life whenever I'd even thought of my Jesus, that experience of Love that had disappeared during my darkness. But now it was so pure, so intense! I wondered if my feet touched the ground. No one was more surprised than I was.*

> *When I had told Jesus that I still loved Him, it hadn't mattered to me if I never experienced this Love again. I had meant that. I'd found out that I loved Him for Himself. It hadn't been because it 'felt' good to love Him. I had come to love Him. He had been my friend. When I was little He had held me. He had wanted to come to me in Communion much more than I had wanted Him, and somehow I knew that even then . . . He had always been there, way down in my heart. There was no reason for living without Him. That's why I had wanted to just fall asleep and not get up during my 'dark night.' I felt genuine affection for Him as a person. No one could ever take His place; we had been through a lot together. Without Him I seemed to have lost*

my own heart.

But things aren't usually what they appear to be. (God) was more present to me during my darkness than He ever had been, but my own (inner) ugliness made it so hard to bear His Presence. What the mystics write is so true. But I didn't know any of it at the time. When I told Him that I still loved Him, for all I knew I would never know His Love as consolation again, and it hadn't mattered. It doesn't matter now. I love Him. God is above all we can know of Him and yet He allows us to possess Him. I know it hurts Him to watch us have to suffer through our own sinfulness so that He can purify us. But He always takes the heaviest part; Jesus did this in His suffering and death on the Cross.

. . . I had no idea what had happened to me . . . Steve told me later that he noticed a difference in me that had been rather sudden. I just seemed calm now and happy. I'm sure I was a lot less crabby. I had every reason in the world to be happy.

The light was back in my life but it had never really gone out. I understood without really being able to explain it in words. When I learned about the Dark Night of the Soul of St. John of the Cross, I understood that this was what I had experienced. All I could do was thank the Lord for allowing me to go through this darkness so that I could become one with the Light in such a marvelous way. It was as if I had never known Jesus before. It seemed as if I was starting all over again, full of new energy and grace. Every difficulty has had that effect on me; I fall in love with Jesus anew each day. But this was incredible, and that abiding sense of His constant Presence has only grown within me since then, like a tiny flame that was transformed into a blazing fire that I can almost sensibly feel. I can never thank Him adequately.

I had experienced times of dryness and darkness many times before in my life. "Darkness" is part of our lives all the time. We deal with it when we have a cold and cannot feel God's presence the way we would like to, or when a dear friend dies suddenly, leaving us reeling in the grief that always follows, or when we are very sick.

Yet I have come to see that every trial is meant to prepare us for union with God both here on earth and in Heaven. Every trial can be a blessing if we decide to cling to Jesus in faith and not give in to the inevitable temptations to abandon Him. A love that is there only in good times is meant to grow into a fire that can never be extinguished. And my experience showed me beyond a shadow of a doubt that it is God's grace alone, with our permission and cooperation, which can make that happen.

Scripture assures us that if we trust, God will never let us go, and experience has taught me that if we put His promises to the test, He will always come through. There is ultimately no way except that of Jesus Himself — the Cross. Suffering comes to everyone but if we are willing to endure it for love of God and others, we will always find ourselves better for it.

In his beautiful poem ***The Dark Night***, mystical Doctor of the Church St. John of the Cross speaks about "the war of the dark night" (***Chapter 24***). He teaches that it is God Himself who works in the soul and we who respond to His purifying light. Because we are sinful creatures, the brightness of God's light seems like darkness to us as we go through these trials that purify our senses and then our spirit, he says, but there is a great advantage to this.

That is because for the enemy, light is darkness. So what God does in the soul is hidden from the devil. God is closer to us than we are to ourselves; there is a "place" within each of us which is unknown even to ourselves, but known only to God. Even when God allows the devil to torment us, the devil cannot know what is going on within us. That means *safety*. And that is exactly what I experienced although I could not understand why at the time. Verse Three of the poem refers to this reason for resting securely in God although all might look bleak on the human level:

> *In that glad night,*
> *In secret, for no one saw me,*
> *Nor did I look at anything,*
> *With no other light or guide*
> *Than the one that burned in my heart;*

I have come to see that, although most difficulties are not the classic Dark Night of the Soul of St. John of the Cross, every difficulty can be a place of hiding in the cleft of the rock, of learning how to trust in the Lord until we are ready to navigate the uncharted waters of the deepest cleansing of our souls. Verse Five of **The Dark Night** states it far more beautifully than I ever could:

> *O guiding night!*
> *O night more lovely than the dawn!*
> *O night that has united*
> *The Lover with His beloved,*
> *Transforming the beloved in her Lover.*

This is the stuff of Heaven. Jesus has turned darkness into light and He loves us so much that He wants to turn all of our personal darknesses into light, one by one, until He takes us through the valley of the shadow of death and unites our hearts to His. Again, St. John of the Cross sums it up in Verse Eight, his final verse:

> *I abandoned and forgot myself,*
> *Laying my face on my Beloved;*
> *All things ceased; I went out from myself,*
> *Leaving my cares*
> *Forgotten among the lilies.*

We don't have to wait for Heaven for that kind of relationship to begin. Like St. John of the Cross and so many others who have gone before us, we can aim for Heaven to begin on earth by surrendering to Jesus in the power of the Holy Spirit, who will bring us to peace and a place of light according to the perfect Will of the Father. I believe that this is what the Lord means when He teaches us to pray "Your Kingdom come" in the ***Our Father.***

The Lord wants our good and wants us united to Him far more than we could ever want Him. He will do His part.

Mary Reveals Her Son

> Lovely Lady, dressed in blue,
> Teach us how to pray!
> God was just your little boy
> And you know the way.
> (Conclusion of a childhood prayer)

Some time ago, when Consolata Father Renato Saudelli ran a little gift shop at the back of the missionary society's U.S. headquarters in Somerset, New Jersey, Jesus and our Blessed Mother revealed their relationship to me in a way that I have never forgotten.

Steve and I would regularly attend after-hours meetings in the gift shop for the prayer group at the Consolata Mission Center. Although we tried to go together, occasionally I would attend meetings myself while Steve stayed home with the children, and vice versa.

Some of the structures have since been removed, including that gift shop, but at the time of this experience, several buildings formed a kind of three-sided courtyard with the gift shop being at the right-most end of one low building, with many acres of open field behind it.

To the shop's left were offices in the same long, low one-story building. Directly across from the building in which the gift shop was located was an old farm house used by the Fathers as a residence, a building which still stands but might have been expanded. When the story I am about to tell occurred, I had not seen the inside of that building because I had never had a reason to enter it. Between both buildings stood another small structure, thus forming a kind of horseshoe with parking in the center, with a well surrounded by bushes in the middle of the cement courtyard.

It seems that very often people can sense another person's gaze, which is why I believe that at one time or another, we've all had the type of experience that I am about to describe. We can almost feel another person's glance staring at us and we unconsciously turn around to find someone with his or her eyes glued to us. And of course they quickly turn away because they have been found out for staring, for whatever reason. Perhaps we have even been the person doing the staring.

Several times as I arrived for a meeting and parked in the courtyard facing the gift shop, I had the distinct feeling that someone was looking out at me from the farm house behind me, particularly from two first-floor windows. Every time I looked over, however, I never saw anyone peering out and I wondered why I was experiencing this very strong sensation that I was being watched. Whoever it was did not seem to move away because that sense continued, but it was not a creepy feeling at all. It just left me wondering.

This particular evening the mystery was solved in a startling way. It seemed that I was the last to arrive that night because cars were parked everywhere. It was dark that night and I was alone, and so I hurried to get out of the car and run into the building where it was warm. I recall that as I stepped out of my car, a very strong gust of wind surprised me, whipping my long coat around and startling me as well. As I held onto my coat and prevented the car door from blowing shut, I was aware of a beautiful, loving presence in the field just behind the shop. Then the wind died down as suddenly as it had begun and everything became very still. Yet there remained a kind of electricity in the air, as if it were charged with energy and light.

Although I could not see around the bend way out in the field, I knew that Mary, our Blessed Mother, was very powerfully present just beyond my view, coming towards me. I could see her in my mind's eye, graceful and illuminated with a living, pure white light. I can still experience her today as clearly as I did that night.

I felt like I was glued to the spot where I stood, unable to move. I finally took a deep breath and realized that I probably had been holding my breath for a little while. It was as if the whole world had stopped in honor of the Blessed Mother. As I held onto my car for support, that sense of someone watching me from behind became noticeably intense at the very same time. I quickly glanced over once more to see if anyone was visible, but as usual I could see no one. The entire experience, over in probably less than a minute, left me astounded but filled with an overpowering joy of the Holy Spirit.

Breathless, I ran into my meeting, unable to concentrate all evening because I was distracted by the continuing sense of Mary's presence outside, filled with this joy that just bubbled up from within me. I was so moved by the whole thing that I found myself unable to talk about it. In fact, I shared it with almost no one until now. I knew that Mary was very much with us and with the Consolata Fathers that night. And I was more curious than ever about who lived in that room in the farm house.

It was not long afterward that the mystery of who was watching me from the farm house was solved. At that time I generally attended 5:30 p.m. daily Mass at the center. For some reason that has long since gone the way of all unnecessary memories, the main chapel where evening Mass was generally held was closed, and we had to use the Fathers' little chapel in their residence.

To my surprise I discovered that the very two windows through which I had sensed someone peering out at me were the windows of a chapel where the Lord Jesus remained in the Blessed Sacrament.

Mary had revealed her Son Jesus in the Blessed Sacrament to me; I experienced their presence together! And how appropriate, since it is through Mary that the incarnate Son of God became flesh and dwelled among us. Mary continues to reveal Him to us constantly, especially in His Real Presence in Eucharist. As His mother and ours, she is constantly pointing the way to Jesus, teaching us how to pray and being completely transparent so that we might see only God.

Mary's apparition at Knock, Ireland, is for me a deep illustration of how our Blessed Lady teaches us to pray. Above all, the prayer *par excellence* is the Mass and that is the lesson she appears to be teaching at Knock. In her appearance in a remote, western Irish village in 1879, Mary is often called Our

Lady of Silence, since in all of her recent apparitions approved by the Church, Mary usually gives a message to the visionaries — in other words, her message is spoken in words that the visionaries audibly hear, or some "secret" messages are given.

That was not so at Knock. Mary appeared behind an altar, upon which a lamb rested. She was the central figure, gazing heavenward with her hands held apart and upward, in the usual position of the priest offering the sacrifice of the Mass. She was dressed as a queen wearing a glittering crown of crosses with a rose in the center of the crown.

According to Mary Purcell in her book **A Woman Clothed with the Sun**, Mary appeared to be praying silently; neither she nor any other figure ever said a word. Above the altar and resting on it was a sacrificial lamb, symbolizing her Son, the Lamb of God. To her right was St. Joseph, appearing to be bowing in reverence, and to her left, St. John the Evangelist, dressed as a bishop wearing a miter.

Interestingly, Purcell points out that none of the visionaries were rapt in ecstasy. They prayed quietly with Mary, whom I believe was telling them symbolically, and telling us through them, to come to her divine Son in the Eucharist. Among the documents of Vatican Council II it is written that ". . . when (Mary) is the subject of preaching and worship she prompts the faithful to come to her Son, to His sacrifice and the love of the Father" (**Lumen Gentium, #65**).

Amazingly close to the beginning and the center of the

mystery of our redemption stands Mary, participating in that redemption by offering her Son on the Cross, as she did symbolically at Knock. Jesus' offering on the Cross in which Mary shared is made present to us in every day and age in every celebration of Eucharist.

In **Redemptoris Mater**, Pope John Paul II refers to **Sermo 25** of St. Augustine of Hippo and points out that Jesus "is of the flesh and blood of Mary." It is she who has preceded us in the journey of faith, she who interceded for the couple at Cana and brought about the Lord's first miracle, and she whose heart broke as she stood at the foot of the Cross in complete surrender and obedience to God's Will.

The pope also specifically states that it is Mary who leads us to her Son in the Eucharist. "The piety of the Christian people has always very rightly sensed a profound link between devotion to the Blessed Virgin and worship of the Eucharist: this is a fact that can be seen in the liturgy of both the West and the East, in traditions of Religious Families, in the modern movements of spirituality, including those for youth, and in the pastoral practice of the Marian shrines. Mary guides the faithful to the Eucharist" (**RM, # 44**).

In her prayer for us at Knock, in her prayer for us as Mother of the Redeemer, Mary holds a unique place, an entirely unique grace, "a high point among all the gifts of grace conferred in the history of man and of the universe" (**RM, # 9**). She is a woman whom we believe was preserved from sin from the moment of her conception in a singular blessing.

But she is also one of us, the "fairest honor of our race," raised from among us as a mediator between ourselves and Jesus by virtue of her role in the Incarnation. She, too, is redeemed by her divine Son. At Knock, Mary is teaching us how to pray in the most efficacious way that God has given us — by being caught up in the offering whereby Jesus gives Himself and us in the Eucharist for the salvation of the world.

Jesus, the high priest, has made of His Church a "kingdom of priests for his God and Father" (**1 Peter 2:5,9**). "The whole community of believers is, as such, priestly. The faithful exercise their baptismal priesthood through their participation, each according to his own vocation, in Christ's mission as priest, prophet and king. Through the Sacraments of Baptism and Confirmation the faithful are 'consecrated to be . . . a holy priesthood' " (**LG 10**). Vatican Council II has emphasized the importance of the role of this "holy priesthood," served by the ministerial priesthood, which is a unique consecration and call from the Lord to shepherd His people.

It is important to say at this point that the exercise of this royal priesthood by the faithful in no way diminishes or threatens the incredible consecration of the Catholic priest in the Sacrament of Holy Orders. The ministry of the priest shares more intimately in the power of the one priesthood of Christ Himself. The priest acts *in persona Christi* — in the person of Christ — when repeating Jesus' words of consecration while celebrating the Eucharist (**CC, #1544-53**).

I think one of the most beautiful explanations of the

essence of what it is to be a Catholic priest was given by a young man who received the extraordinary privilege of being ordained but a few hours before his death in New York at the age of 24. His name was Father Eugene Hamilton.

In *A Priest Forever: The Life of Father Eugene Hamilton*, Father Benedict J. Groeschel has put together a moving testimony of what it is to be a Catholic priest. In Father Gene's own words, a priest "must be one who loves and can bring the love that Christ has to others" (*pg, 35*). That sacrificial love, grounded in the Cross of Christ, does not end with death. Although Father Gene never offered Mass or heard a single Confession, he remains a priest forever. What an awesome call.

In his book *In Search of the Sacred*, philosopher Josef Pieper examines, among other things, "What Makes a Priest?" To be an ordained priest is much more than just being able to perform a specific set of tasks, he states. A priest is dedicated and consecrated to God — offered totally in self-sacrifice, and set apart from the world by renouncing "explicitly and perma-nently the common standards of life . . . vow(ing) himself to the exclusive service of God" (*p. 61*).

"The essential distinction of the priest . . . consists in a special spiritual authority invested in him through his ordina-tion, a *potestas sacra* (sacred power), in the Council's words," Pieper continues. The ordained priest is most identified with the person of Christ "in his power to celebrate the Eucharist, *in persona Christi* and for the universal Church" (*p. 64*).

The priest need not search frantically for his specific "identity", Pieper comments earlier in the chapter entitled "The Sacred and Its Negation." When the sense of the sacred disappears, when belief in the Real Presence is denied, it only stands to reason that there is no need for the sacred power of an ordained priest. The two — faith in Christ's Real Presence and the power of the ordained priesthood to consecrate ordinary bread and wine into the Body and Blood of Christ *in persona Christi* — are intimately linked and dependent upon each other. And the very sacramental life of the Church, of every man, woman and child who seeks to live within the Body of Christ, depends ultimately on the ministry of those whom Jesus Himself calls and empowers for the sake of His people.

In our day in particular, belief in the Lord's Real Presence is under especially heavy attack. That makes sense if destruction of the Catholic faith is one's object. St. Thomas Aquinas and the Church have consistently taught that the Eucharist is the summit and source of our faith, the place in our faith where the veil is the thinnest between heaven and earth. I am certain that the devil — the "serpent" — hates it most of all.

Because of the priest's intimate association with the Eucharist, and the entire sacramental life of God's people, it is no wonder that the priesthood is under similar attack, especially obvious in today's scandals in the U.S. It would seem that all of us need to reclaim the spiritual riches that are ours, stop looking for the "highest places" at table, and remember that we are all on the same side — our Lord's side.

I believe that Mary, who crushed the head of the serpent, teaches us to pray by calling us first and foremost to participation in the Eucharist, to hearing God's Word and receiving her Son in adoration, reverence and worship. It seems to me that her apparition at Knock means even more for us today than it did 100 years ago.

Above all, in our own time of unspeakable evils and disrespect for the gift of life that is from God — abortion, infanticide, nuclear weapons, euthanasia, violence, "religious" terrorism, genetic experimentation, embryonic stem cell research and more — I believe that Mary will lead us to her Son most powerfully through the Eucharist.

For every celebration of Eucharist has made it clearer to me that we have not been privileged to know the truth, Who is Jesus, for ourselves. Called to be a "royal priesthood" by virtue of our Baptism, we are to offer spiritual sacrifices with our great High Priest, be strengthened by receiving His Body and Blood, and are then commanded to go out to all the world and

spread the Good News of the Gospel by word *and* deeds wherever God sends us.

I believe that Mary is teaching us — the members of her Son's royal priesthood and ministerial priesthood together — to begin at the Eucharistic table, and especially if we have any doubts of her Son's Real Presence, she will reveal Him to us.

I Am The Lord Your God

> The fear of the LORD is the beginning of wisdom;
> prudent are all who live by it.
> Your praise endures forever.
>
> (*Psalm 111:10*)

"Fear" and "fear of the Lord" are two very different things. The Lord chose to teach me about the vast differences between them in two separate lessons that made a deep and lasting impression on me.

On a family vacation years ago on Hilton Head Island, South Carolina, the Lord provided me with a very graphic experience of fear. My family and I decided to take a walk through a park near our rented condo in Sea Pines. A walkway is built over a swamp so that tourists can take a self-guided tour and observe the wildlife in the tropical wetlands below, including baby alligators. It was fascinating, and we thought quite safe, almost like being in a zoo where we are shielded from the dangers. That was not quite the case. As we reached the end of the ramp, I stopped and stood with my hand on the railing for a few more minutes. Had I known what I was standing next to, I would have moved away very quickly.

When I joined my family beyond the ramp on dry ground, I looked back into the trees. I was focusing into the distance for awhile until I realized that there appeared to be something obstructing my view. So I focused on the foreground and felt myself getting the chills. Within only a few feet of where I had just stood was the largest spider and web that I had ever seen. Without exaggeration, the web was several feet in diameter with a huge, perfectly-camouflaged spider sitting motionless in the center. I gasped as I realized that I had stood so close to it, totally unaware of its presence. It blended so well into the green background. I shuddered as I saw that my hand had rested on the railing within inches of the end of that enormous web.

Not particularly fond of spiders, especially their sticky webs, I experienced pure and simple fear, coupled with a healthy desire to get myself and my family as far away from this creature as I could.

The Lord Jesus also taught me about fear of the Lord, the gift of the Holy Spirit, in a very powerful way. He taught me about awe and wonder and respect, all movements of the heart that open our hearts to experience the divine as God is, and not as we imagine Him to be.

Jesus taught me this lesson through another encounter with Him in the Blessed Sacrament, and I believe He chose this particular way for a particular set of reasons. For we live in a world that ridicules faith, let alone faith in a Savior who miraculously makes Himself completely present as spiritual Food. It is a world that in the last several centuries particularly, has rushed headlong into a spiritual abyss of unbelief and disrespect for life itself, of which God is the source.

On retreat in Staten Island, New York, many years ago, I was exploring the retreat house shortly after I arrived. I came upon a small chapel and was surprised to find no kneelers,

Holy Ground

simply a room with windows facing me as I walked in, soft carpeting on the floors and a very "busy" stone wall to my right, with an altar before it. I recall seeing a tabernacle light burning softly in the corner of the room.

Accustomed to genuflecting out of respect to Jesus in the Blessed Sacrament, I entered the tiny room and looked for the tabernacle. But it was impossible to find. The mosaic wall was so ornate and confusing that despite searching it, I could not locate a tabernacle and wondered why there would be a light burning.

I seemed to sense the Real Presence of Jesus somewhere but I didn't genuflect. Instead I started to walk briskly toward the windows to look outside, much as I would in an ordinary classroom or in my home or in any place where the Lord's Real Presence is not reserved. I should have reverenced the altar as I passed it, but didn't.

All at once, I was overwhelmed by a sense that I find impossible to fully describe: a tangible sense of Jesus' loving Presence that literally held me in mid-step and compelled me to kneel down in adoration. I was puzzled and surprised by this sacred sense that completely filled the room, reminding me very much of Jesus' lesson many years before on how to pray the *Our Father.*

The Holy Spirit gave me an unquestionable inner assurance that Jesus was indeed present, that I was on holy ground. Still confused and literally quite shaken, I scanned the wall more carefully and asked the Lord to please tell me where He was.

Right before me, within a few feet, was a very well-con-
cealed tabernacle, artfully blended into the swirling patterns and
shapes of the wall, not unlike the large green spider I had
encountered hiding in the swamp. No wonder I couldn't see
the tabernacle! It seemed deliberately designed to be hardly
noticeable, a statement that was glaringly at odds with the
experience of the trembling young woman kneeling alone
before the Lord Jesus in the Blessed Sacrament.

Jesus wrapped me up in His love as He said volumes to my
heart without a single word. I understood the gift of fear of the
Lord as I never had before. I knew that it is impossible to truly
encounter the living God without being moved to some degree
of awe and wonder in His Presence. And because He is Love, to
be in awe of Him is to be more deeply in love with Him.

Jesus tells us in *1 John 4:18* that "perfect love drives out
fear." There was a world of difference between my fearful
encounter with a large spider and this awe-inspiring and humbling encounter with the living God in the Blessed Sacrament.
I ran from the spider in fear; I "ran" inwardly toward Jesus in
love even while trembling because of the confidence that the
gifts of piety and fear of the Lord provided.

The Catechism of the Catholic Church lists the seven
gifts of the Holy Spirit — wisdom, understanding, counsel,
fortitude, knowledge, piety, and fear of the Lord (*#1831*). It
explains that these gifts complete and perfect the virtues of
those who receive them, and they "make the faithful docile in
readily obeying divine inspirations."

Holy fear of the Lord doesn't mean being afraid of God in the same sense that I was afraid of the spider. It means a deep respect for God, and for Catholics, it means a deep respect for Jesus in the celebration of the Eucharist and in the reserved Blessed Sacrament. Many no longer believe in Jesus' Eucharistic Presence and numbers of young people today have not been adequately taught that He comes at every celebration of Mass to be wholly, completely with us at the words of consecration said by the priest. Heaven meets with earth in every Mass.

As I knelt before Him that day, as I had every day before that, it continues to be confirmed very quietly that Jesus is not just "one of the guys;" He is God. Our bodily expressions of respect — kneeling, bowing, genuflecting, folding our hands in prayer — are necessary for us to love God with our whole selves.

The British scholar C.S. Lewis, a non-Catholic, knew about that. The renowned critic, novelist and author of more than 40 books constantly displayed a brilliant understanding of the human psyche in the light of Christian faith. In fact, he obviously believed that the devils themselves know it and use it to impede the spiritual growth of those who pray.

In ***The Screwtape Letters***, a book written as a series of fictional "letters" from senior devil Screwtape to his nephew Wormwood, a junior demon whom he is mentoring, we hear how the minions of Hell understand us better than we understand ourselves. Screwtape's descriptions of humans are less than complimentary as he makes suggestions on how to tempt those who pray. But there is great wisdom in his "insights", or rather, in Lewis' having put it on Screwtape's lips.

In Chapter 4, Screwtape instructs his young charge to tempt humans to think that they need not use their bodies when praying, reminding Wormwood that humans are merely "animals" and that their bodies and souls are intimately connected. A worshiping body "affects" a worshiping soul.

I ask myself to this day: Why would anyone want to hide the tabernacle which holds the Lord Jesus? Released in July 2000, the revised **General Instruction of the Roman Missal** (**No. 314**), on reservation of the Eucharist, recommends that, "In accordance with the structure of each church and legitimate local customs, the Most Blessed Sacrament should be reserved in a tabernacle in a part of the church which is noble, prominent, visible, beautifully decorated, and suitable for prayer." The **GIRM** offers locating the tabernacle in the sanctuary, apart from the altar of sacrifice, as the first option. The **GIRM** continues, stating that the tabernacle can also be placed "even in another chapel suitable for adoration and private prayer of the faithful, and which is integrally connected with the church and conspicuous to the faithful"(**No. 315**). Too many tabernacles are literally hidden in corners and inconspicuous places off to the side in so many of our "updated" churches today. As regards the Blessed Sacrament, the constant teaching of the Church is echoed in the words of Pope Paul VI:

> The Catholic Church has always offered and still offers
> to the sacrament of the Eucharist the cult of adoration,

not only during Mass, but also outside of it, reserving the consecrated hosts with the utmost care, exposing them to the solemn veneration of the faithful, and carrying them in procession." (***Mysterium Fidei 56*** *in* ***The Catechism of the Catholic Church***, ***#1378***).

Pope John Paul II has reaffirmed that teaching and developed it repeatedly.

Also, I cannot help but wonder why in so many ways we Catholics appear to have lost so much respect for the Lord's Eucharistic Presence during the Mass and in the tabernacle. Have we lost even all common sense? Who would dare refuse the Lord the honor or the glory due His name (***Rev. 15:4***)? This was certainly not the intention of Vatican Council II, but it does appear that some have misinterpreted several of the Council's suggestions and emphasized the interpretation of the Eucharist as a meal over and above the fact that Christ is really present, and that He does come to us individually as well as collectively. That beautiful balance can only be achieved by the power of the Holy Spirit, and Jesus' Real Presence cannot be sacrificed for a sacred meal. Christ's Real Presence and the sacred meal are both irreducible parts of the Eucharist.

The awe and wonder of encountering the divine, most often subtle and gentle like the whispering wind in which Elijah recognized the Spirit of God (***1 Kings 19:12***), demand a response in faith. That is where our answer lies. I truly believe that we need to ask the Holy Spirit to strengthen the theological virtues of faith, hope and charity, as well as to reawaken the gifts of fear of the Lord and piety within us, with all of His marvelous gifts. Given to us by a generous God at our Baptism and Confirmation, the gifts are meant to grow within us.

In his 1925 classic book on spirituality, **Christ the Life of the Soul**, Benedictine Abbot Columba Marmion teaches that the gifts of piety and fear of the Lord complement each another. Piety regulates our attitude toward God, "the blending of adoration, respect and profound reverence towards the Divine Majesty; of love, confidence, tenderness, perfect abandonment and holy liberty in presence of Him who is our Heavenly Father."

There are also two kinds of fear of God: servile fear and filial fear. Servile fear "thinks only of the chastisement due to sin;" filial fear avoids sin because it offends God, but it remains imperfect as long as there remains any fear of punishment. Fear of the Lord, that which was present in Jesus, "evinces itself by adoration and is altogether holy," a "perfect, reverential fear."

"This is the reverence that the Spirit places within our souls; He keeps it there but in mingling it, by the gift of piety, with that love and filial tenderness which results from our Divine adoption and makes us cry out to God: 'Father!' " (**pp. 122-23**).

Without a sense of the holiness and awesomeness of God, obedience to His commandments and to His demands becomes a terrible burden. Fear of the Lord, with its marvelous blend of confidence and respect, makes doing God's Will a joy rather than

a burden. We are in right relationship when we fear the Lord and that is the foundation of a solid relationship with Him.

It is only with the gifts of the Holy Spirit that we can respond to God's Presence in reverence and in love without fear, simply for who He is — the glorious Lord who is Love revealed in the person of the risen Lord Jesus, remaining with us through the power of the Holy Spirit in the Church, in His Word and above all, in His Eucharistic Presence.

Dusty 'Hats'

Steve had to make a winter business trip to London back in the 1980s, and I was fortunate enough to be able to accompany him for 10 wonderful days. I was thrilled that I was going to the country of one of my favorite saints, Thomas More, and of one of my favorite Christian authors, C.S. Lewis. I had always wanted to visit England and here was an opportunity not to be missed.

The trip made me acutely aware of how very much I am a child of my own culture and time, an American living in a fast-paced world in a young country with a very short history of only 200 years. As such, it is easy to become shortsighted about things like time and eternity.

Visiting the elaborate tombs in Westminster Abbey and ancient artifacts in the British Museum made history so very real in ways that a McDonald's mentality was incapable of producing artificially. There is nothing that can substitute for the feel of the earth beneath one's feet when that earth contains such a rich and varied history, even if only in memory. It was like touching my roots, in a way, everywhere I went.

A special treat was visiting Canterbury to experience the roots of my parish family here in New Jersey, to touch the places where St. Augustine of Canterbury walked and lived when years were comprised of only three numbers rather than four. But perhaps one of the most startling moments occurred quite by surprise one day as a woman in Westminster Cathedral, the Catholic cathedral of London, gave me a short, impromptu tour of the building after Mass one morning.

The tour of the crypt beneath the main church was fascinating in that I had not ever seen the tombs of past cardinals and bishops placed throughout the sacred space where Mass was held on a daily basis. Even in St. Patrick's Cathedral in New York City, the crypt is hidden below the main altar and is inaccessible to the casual visitor.

As I was led to the tomb of Cardinal Henry Edward Manning who had died about 100 years before my visit, a free-standing sarcophagus intricately carved with his sleeping image, I could not help but look up because the ceiling of the room was quite low, so low that I could probably have touched it if I were standing next to the tomb.

Above the stone casket was a large red velvet "hat" signifying his office as cardinal, a "galero". It was limp and covered with a very thick, heavy black layer of dust. I have never seen dust so thick in my entire life. Although it appeared to have been handsome in its day, the galero was in fact disintegrating before our eyes.

All at once it became so clear in a new and deeper way just how trivial all of our honors are here in this life. This symbol of the man's office was turning into dust in a mere 100 years. All of our glory fades like the passing flowers, so quickly and so silently, as the days blend one into another and unique opportunities to make a difference for the better in the lives of those God puts into our path offer themselves once, and then forever hold their peace.

And I prayed for him and for all priests, especially those in high office, because it is so easy to become caught up in the false values of power and glory. For here before me was myself and every one of us someday — drawn inexorably back into the heart of the Lord from whence we came, completely powerless to fight back, no matter how hard we try. We do belong to the Lord in life and in death, whether we acknowledge it or not, and I love Him.

Shortly after returning to the states, I was in St. Patrick's Cathedral, probably near Christmas as I especially enjoy New York City during the Christmas season, and it is very likely that we went in for a visit during the holiday season.

For some reason I was walking alone around the main altar and came to a halt at the white marble staircase that winds its way down beneath the main altar. It dawned on me for the first time since I had visited the cathedral that the cardinals must have been buried there just like in England, and I peered down with a new sense of respect.

The memory of the dusty "hat" popped into my mind and I gazed up, almost as an afterthought, because it did not seem possible that these hats could have been hung in this cathedral. The ceiling is about eight stories high.

To my surprise there they were — four galeros suspended so far above me that I had to hold my head all the way back to be able to even see them. I had never noticed them before, I guess because I had never known to look for them. I had to go halfway around the world to find out that they even existed. According to Friar of the Atonement Brother Denis Sennett, cathedral archivist, the custom of placing a galero over the tomb of a cardinal or archbishop was ended some time ago, although within this century.

I spent a while standing there looking up, noting the contrast between the hat I had watched falling apart almost before my eyes in the crypt in London and the relative newness of this most recently hung hat, and I was all the more impressed with the fleeting quality of our lives, the shortness of our days, as the psalmist says. In just 100 years this hat and its companions would look the same.

I experienced that day an indescribable oneness with Terrence Cardinal Cooke, who is buried in the cathedral and for whom I have a particular affection, and with all those who have gone before me.

It didn't matter how or where they lived, no matter how long ago they died, no matter how "important" was their station in life, or how lowly it was. I was given a tiny glimpse of the Kingdom of God in a new light, the light that is Christ who is the same yesterday, today and tomorrow and brings us all into His one Body.

It was good to experience this taste of my mortality so personally, because it put me in touch with the love of God and His people in a more honest way. Rather than feeling fearful, I experienced deep gratitude for the wisdom given me in that sacred space.

O Lord, please teach us to number our days aright, to recognize our utter dependence upon your love and mercy! Please see that we might always we blessed with these sacred spaces and consecrated people to bring You to us at Your Eucharistic table.

CHAPTER 21

Forgiveness

*I*n his beautiful and profound reflection on suffering, ***Salvifici Dolores***, Pope John Paul II begins by affirming what we all know — "in whatever form, suffering seems to be, and is, almost inseparable from man's earthly existence" (***#3***).

It is what we do with that suffering that makes all the difference in time and eternity. Jesus has always blessed and taught me about Himself best through suffering, and it was through another episode of deep suffering that He taught me that forgiveness is everything. It finds its meaning in the Cross and in divine Love. My life was changed forever once more, because the lessons in the power of forgiveness and of the Cross which Jesus had been teaching to me constantly through-out my life came into even clearer focus. And I understood more than ever the beauty of death in the Lord, for it is simply ceasing to breathe here on earth and beginning to "breathe" the pure light of Love in Heaven.

I had been admitted to Lankenau Hospital in Philadelphia right after New Year's Day in 1990 for what was supposed to be a routine laser hysterectomy. It was not.

I was there because a large ovarian cyst had been located for the second time in as many years, and although I had had major surgery once already, it appeared that the problem had recurred. I also had other problems and it had been decided that a hyster-ectomy was best. If I did not have one, I risked having to go through surgery again when more problems occurred.

I was supposed to be up and on my feet within two weeks,

ready to go back to school at the end of January, using my mid-
semester break from my studies for a master's degree at
Villanova University and then just getting on with life. But an
ominous sense hung over me before I went into the hospital, and
I recall breaking down in tears at my sister Nancy's house as we
tried to celebrate Christmas as a family. Not being one generally
frightened of what was supposed to be a routine procedure, and
especially having had a million and one illnesses since childhood,
it was atypical behavior for me and my family knew that. They
were upset too, because they must have realized that I sensed that
serious problems were on the horizon, just a few days away.

When I awoke in the intensive care unit after surgery with
Steve standing by my side, holding my hand, I knew by the
amount of pain I was experiencing that something was very
wrong. I also knew it immediately by the color of Steve's face,
and although I cannot see very much without my glasses, I
know Steve very well and I knew that things were bad.

Despite my grogginess I insisted that he tell me everything,
which he did. What we had expected was only the tip of the
iceberg. I had been in surgery for 11 and a half hours, rather
than the expected two and a half, because there had been
tumors everywhere in the abdomen. My doctors at first believed that my condition was non-malignant. However, Steve
was told that I would need chemotherapy anyway and that even
with chemo, the prognosis was not very good. He was told
that the usual course at that time of the fairly rare disease they
thought I had was that patients usually survived about two years

at most, with recurring tumors and repeated surgeries until there was nothing else that could be removed without causing death. Steve told me that a lot of "parts" had been removed already because of the extent of the tumors.

My first reaction was a profound peace, and I found myself reassuring Steve that we would do what we had to do. It was pure grace and I recognized that even at the time. After all, Jesus had been with me when I went into surgery and He certainly was still with me. I experienced a deep, inner strength and hope. The Lord had never let me down before. I would take it one day at a time.

That was just the beginning. I knew I had a long road ahead of me but at least it was not cancer, or so we thought. About four days past surgery my doctors came into the room while Steve was there and tried to tell us as best as they could that it *was* cancer, that a malignancy had been found. We were totally stunned. I'll never forget the look on one of the doctor's faces. He was so young and he looked so pale, almost gray. I could tell he had me dead and buried, and he didn't have the experience of having told many people that they were going to die (although they were not saying that in words), so his expression could not hide the grief he felt. I felt my heart going out to him and I will never forget his face, even though I do not know his name. I pray for him, that he remains as compassionate as he seemed that afternoon.

Even as this team of physicians stood all around my room and seemed to be telling me that we were dealing with a very serious or maybe even hopeless situation, especially if it was ovarian cancer, the peace in my spirit remained steady. I felt no fear, no numbness, no horror at that time, just that profound peace, for the Holy Spirit was comforting me in wonderful ways. Everyone else appeared to be much more upset than I was. I knew even then that I was not in denial; Jesus was inwardly assuring me that He would take care of me and I believed Him.

Someone was definitely praying for me, praying for us. I reassured Steve that we did not yet know what kind of cancer we were dealing with, so why give up now. If it were really bad, if it were ovarian, once we knew that for sure we would deal with it. But we did not know, so why worry? Jesus is right in *Mt. 6:34*. Today has trouble enough of its own; why be concerned about tomorrow? I know it was grace.

Steve was staying in a guest room in the hospital at the time and when he went back to his room, he prayed. When we next saw each other, probably later that day, he told me that he had opened to a reading that had literally jumped out of the page at him. It was a reading that Steve had often opened to in the Bible when we prayed together before that day. We have grown very comfortable praying with each other over the years. As part of a prayer group, we'd both learned how to pray as a couple and it came quite naturally by this point in our lives. Thank God it did.

I believe that the Bible in Steve's room was a Gideon Bible. He opened to *Isaiah 37:30-32 (NAB* version follows).

> This shall be a sign for you:
>> this year you shall eat the aftergrowth,
>> next year, what grows of itself;

But in the third year, sow and reap,
     plant vineyards and eat their fruit!

For almost 12 years we had often opened to that reading during our prayer together and it made no sense. It did not make any sense now either and we were surprised that it came up again.

However, the pages of this particular Bible were configured differently than our **New American Bible**. In our Bible, Chapter 37 ends on the right side of the two facing pages when the book was open, so that in order to read Chapter 38 one has to turn the page. In the Bible Steve read, Chapters 37 and 38 were visible with the book open, so he had continued on to read Chapter 38 after finishing Chapter 37. It narrates the story of the sickness and recovery of King Hezekiah, including the king's prayer of thanksgiving.

Hezekiah pleads with the Lord to let him live longer when he is faced with death. He reminds God that he, Hezekiah, has served God faithfully. And the Lord promises to let him live 15 more years, giving him a sign by turning the sun backwards — by reversing time — to prove that Hezekiah's health would be restored and he would live a while longer.

The king's **Hymn of Thanksgiving** is very moving. He thanks the Lord from the depths of his heart for granting his prayer. The **New American Bible** version reads as follows:
     Once I said,
          'In the noontime of life I must depart!
     To the gates of the nether world I shall be consigned

for the rest of my years.'
I said, 'I shall see the LORD no more
   in the land of the living.
No longer shall I behold my fellow men
   among those who dwell in the world.'
My dwelling, like a shepherd's tent,
   is struck down and borne away from me;
You have folded up my life, like a weaver
   who severs the last thread.
Day and night you give me over to torment;
   I cry out until the dawn.
Like a lion he breaks all my bones;
   [day and night you give me over to torment].
Like a swallow I utter shrill cries;
   I moan like a dove.
My eyes grow weak, gazing heavenward:
   O Lord, I am in straits; be my surety!

What am I to say or tell him?
   He has done it!
I shall go on through all my years
   despite the bitterness of my soul.
Those live whom the LORD protects,
   yours . . . the life of my spirit.
You have given me health and life;
   thus is my bitterness transformed into peace.
You have preserved my life
   from the pit of destruction,
When you cast behind your back
   all my sins.
For it is not the nether world that gives you thanks,

nor death that praises you.
Neither do those who go down into the pit
   await your kindness.
The living, the living give you thanks,
   as I do today.
Fathers declare to their sons,
   O God, your faithfulness.
The LORD is our savior;
   we shall sing to stringed instruments
In the house of the LORD
   all the days of our life. *(Isaiah 38:10-20)*

This prayer appears in the **Liturgy of the Hours**, Tuesday, Week Two. Although it still is difficult for me to read because I relive my suffering of that time every time I pray it, something beautiful happens to me each time as well. I also recall what happened that very difficult day in our lives. Steve had received a very positive sense that the words of **Isaiah 38**, the Lord's promise to extend Hezekiah's life, were somehow also meant for me. As I read those words, I was also deeply moved as we came to understand what they meant for us.

Incredibly, we both knew that the Lord was going to give me some more time. It was as if the verses of **Isaiah 38** were spoken directly to us. It must have been grace. Just the fact that we both received that same strong sense of peace is incredible in itself. And we understood why we had opened to Chapter 37 so many times, for so many years previous to that awful day. Our faithfulness in prayer had prepared us for this moment of deep crisis, for the day when Steve would pick up a particular Bible and see the reading that was meant to console us and convey God's promise to us. When we needed to hear from the Lord, not only had we learned how to listen, but we were able to discern what He was saying to us — as a couple. It was a beautiful moment, one that gave us a very deep peace, even though we did not have any details and things seemed quite bleak at the time.

A few nights later, I was awakened from a light sleep, which is not surprising in a hospital. Sleeping in any hospital is difficult because they are very noisy places, plus I still was in a great deal of pain. This time, however, I was gently awakened by the Lord Jesus.

I awoke to "see" Him above and before me, as I was connected to countless IVs and pumps. I opened my eyes and He was there, but I could not physically "see" Him. I experienced His physical presence without seeing Him with my bodily eyes. Jesus' Presence was powerfully intense and holy. It was as if I was looking upon spiritual fire, if that is possible. It seems to me that there is no way to doubt that it is the Lord when He manifests Himself this way. It was really awesome — very solemn — an experience of great "majesty" as St. Teresa of Avila might say. In her autobiography, she seems to describe this type of vision (*Chapter 27*), but my own experience differed in the circumstances (critical illness) and the kind of lesson the Lord came to teach me, one that most people associate with approaching death.

Not a word needed to be spoken. The conversation was one of Heart to heart. Jesus impressed the most important thing on my mind and heart that I believe He has ever taught me.

He spoke no words; He *was* forgiveness. People have described "near death" experiences where their entire lives flashed before their eyes in a split second. What happened to me was different. It was not like a movie where every moment of my life went by at accelerated speed. Instead, it was impressed on me that in the end, it is mercy and forgiveness that are of the utmost importance, for God's love ultimately manifests itself to us most beautifully as forgiveness. Jesus' words from the Cross — "Father forgive them, they know not what they do" (***Luke 23:34***) — summarize the gift of the Father as salvation by the forgiveness of our sins (***The Canticle of Zechariah, Luke 1:77***). I understood more than I ever had that we *must* forgive others as He forgives us in order to join Him when our lives here are over and our eternal life begins. I knew the beauty of forgiveness in a deeper way, how it frees us from Satan's power, and how forgiveness will determine which events will flash before our minds as we "stand" before Jesus at the end of our lives.

It seems to me that if we have been graced to forgive those who "trespass against us," and therefore have been forgiven by God as stated so clearly in the ***Our Father***, then we will be free and more open to Him when He looks lovingly upon us as our merciful judge. For Jesus' redemptive love covers all of our sinfulness and weaknesses. I knew that as I gazed on Him that night.

My whole being was held captive by Jesus, and I was being loved immensely, like a flower petal softly floating on an infinite sea of forgiveness and mercy. Jesus' presence was that of complete and absolute forgiveness, and infinite kindness. With

incomparable and astonishing tenderness, like a Father caress-
ing a tiny baby, Jesus "showed" me His loving forgiveness as He
surrendered His life to death on the Cross for us. It was as if I
looked for a brief moment into the secret abyss of love and
mercy and compassion and forgiveness of His Heart, at the
very moment that He surrendered up His life into the hands of
our Father. I was graced to be "with Him" in a certain sense,
not in His suffering but in His spirit of surrender. And I
understood in that brief moment that *forgiveness is everything.*

The best word that I can use to try to describe this moment is
"transparent". There is nowhere to hide when the Lord Jesus
comes this way. At that time, there was a small annoyance on my
mind and I sensed that Jesus "smiled" with obvious joy as I realized
how trivial it really was and released it to Him. I knew that by His
amazing grace I had been forgiven and had forgiven others as best I
could at that time. Right then and there, I was ready to go home
with Jesus if He wanted me to do so. It was the most peaceful
moment of my life up until then. There was absolutely no fear.

I am reminded here of St. Teresa of Avila's words on death
written in her autobiography. "Now death seems to me to be
the easiest thing for anyone who serves God," she says, "for in
a moment the soul finds that it is freed from this prison and
brought to rest." (***Chapter 38***) It seems to me that death
comes very gently for those who love God and surrender to
Him, that it is simply a transition from breathing here on earth
to breathing the pure breath of the Holy Spirit in heaven.

Although I wanted very much to live to raise my family, it

was when I realized that I would gladly accompany Jesus immediately, that I knew that I would be "all right." The Lord Jesus told me inwardly without words that He would be my "doctor", just as He had impressed the knowledge of forgiveness upon my mind. That is why I know that it was the Lord who sent me the excellent doctors who took a chance and saved my life. I almost immediately began to drift off to sleep, His glorious presence still above and before me, remaining as my consolation. I felt like a tiny baby being rocked to sleep in my mother's arms, safe and secure and loved. Jesus' Presence has often had that effect on me if He awakens me from sleep; once He has said or done what He came for, I am so much at peace that I cannot help but drift off into sleep.

I treasured the memory of the Lord's visit deep in my heart and could not stop thanking Him for it. I knew from the moment the Lord reassured me that somehow I was going to be all right. No one else knew it yet but I did, and that confidence remained unshaken somewhere deep within me throughout the rest of our ordeal.

Sometime shortly after that we were told that the cancer was not ovarian but rather the primary site was the appendix, a very rare cancer but far more treatable. The young resident had a smile on his face. At least my prognosis was not as grim as it might have been had it been an ovarian cancer; we were being given a little more time together, even if it would be very difficult and possibly only a few years. Jesus went on to prove that with God nothing is impossible — absolutely nothing. He had really meant that I would be "all right."

The Lord recently confirmed the message of forgiveness and merciful love He had impressed on my heart so many years before, and of the power of the most important prayer of the gathered Church, the Eucharist. At a regular Sunday celebration of the Eucharist in my parish, I was one of the Eucharistic ministers gathered around the altar in the sanctuary. Just before distribution of Communion, all at once and without any warning, it appeared as if the consecrated Hosts, the chalices holding the Precious Blood and the entire altar were bathed in a beautiful, intense light that miraculously did not hurt my eyes. I was held captive as I had been when Jesus had come to me in my hospital room. Simultaneously, something was happening inwardly that left a permanent impression on my soul.

Again without words, I recognized Jesus in the breaking of the bread as did the disciples on the road to Emmaus, and it was the lesson of forgiveness that Jesus repeated and expanded upon. I knew that all sin, anger, hatred, resentment, violence and fear — that *all* evil stopped on the Cross and therefore stops here, in the sacrifice of Jesus Who is completely present at every Eucharist and Who makes that grace present to us in our own day.

The power for world peace is here. The power to mend all relationships, to bring incomparable joy, to experience the peace and true justice in community that we were created to experience, is all here. The answers to wars and prejudice are here because the grace to change hearts is here, because *Jesus is here*!

In his encyclical letter **Dives in Misericordia (The Mercy** *of God*), Pope John Paul II teaches that unless justice is present with the merciful love of Jesus, interpersonal and social relationships will not make for a more "human" world. "Forgiveness demonstrates the presence in the world of the love which is more powerful than sin. Forgiveness is also the fundamental condition for reconciliation, not only in the relationship of God with man, but also in relationships between people. A world from which forgiveness was eliminated would be nothing but a world of cold and unfeeling justice, in the name of which each person would claim his or her own rights *vis-à-vis* others; the various kinds of selfishness latent in man would transform life and human society into a system of oppression of the weak by the strong, or into an arena of permanent strife between one group and another . . . Thus, the fundamental structure of justice always enters into the sphere of mercy," he states (*DM # 14*).

The way of forgiveness is the way that God the Father has made for us to follow. That forgiveness is made available to us in a special way in the Sacrament of Reconciliation and most perfectly in the Sacrament of the Eucharist.

The Christian community that gathers around the Eucharistic table cannot live without merciful love and forgiveness, which find their roots in "the mystery of the mercy of God Himself as revealed in Jesus Christ." (*DM # 14*) The grace of forgiveness is present in the sacrifice of the Mass and in the Body and Blood of Jesus at every single Mass, and it is pure gift. As I stood near that altar, I knew that it is a gift that He eagerly waits for us to take, and live.

Healing in His Time

> May He support us all the day long,
> till the shades lengthen and the evening comes,
> and the busy world is hushed
> and the fever of life is over and our work is done.
> Then in His mercy
> may He give us a safe lodging
> and a holy rest
> and peace at the last.
>
> **Cardinal John Henry Newman, Sermon 20**

One of the greatest heartaches during my time of hospitalization at Lankenau was that I was unable to receive the Lord Jesus in the Eucharist on a daily basis at first. At the time of my life when I most needed to receive Jesus, with all of His healing power, and to maintain my connection with the rest of my sisters and brothers in the Body of Christ, I was not able to.

At the time, Lankenau hospital was served by a local Catholic parish that didn't have a large number of Eucharistic ministers, and the parish policy was that Catholic patients were seen once upon admission and Communion distributed only on Sundays. But Jesus took care of me through the pastoral sensitivity of my local pastor at the time, Msgr. William A. Capano, who has since died, and to whom I am eternally grateful for this.

Msgr. Capano was aware of my love for the Lord in the Eucharist and that I attended Mass daily. Although I was more than 50 miles and several dioceses away from home, he allowed Steve to bring the Lord Jesus to me daily, except for Sundays, after he learned that I was unable to receive Eucharist through the local channels. It was a wonderful thing for Steve and me to share each day. And Steve appreciated the sacred time when he drove the hour-long trip daily to the hospital from central New Jersey.

According to one of the most current chaplains at Lankenau, the situation was addressed by the Archdiocese of Philadelphia, with a new system spreading the burden of hospital coverage to several parishes. I am so relieved because I know how unbearable it was to not be able to receive my Lord for even just a week or so. I could have died during that week.

I left Lankenau after 36 days, 30 pounds lighter than when I entered. I was already thin when I went into the hospital; I was so weak that I could barely stand or walk when I left. I had had my first course of chemotherapy and I was very, very sick. From the way things looked, I was not going to be all right in the very near future but that was okay. There is something about the incredible hope that the Lord gives; it was there underneath the surface, strong and alive in my soul, giving me strength for the ordeal to come.

The road ahead of us was still a very a long one. Incredible complications set in after my initial surgery, and I had several more surgical procedures and surgeries over the coming year. What followed was one of the hardest years of my life because it affected so many people for such a long period of time — my husband, children, family and friends. It didn't seem like I was improving very much at all.

No new tumors were appearing as we had expected them to, but the chemotherapy was making me very ill. I was constantly nauseous, unable to eat very much and spent a good part of the year in and out of hospitals. Each chemo session took five full days as an in-patient, so I received treatments in our two local hospitals. For days after chemo, I couldn't see well even wearing my glasses and when I was finally beginning to feel a tiny bit better, it was time to go back in again. By my sixth treatment the dosage was cut down because I couldn't tolerate it anymore; by that point I had no good days at all. I was just constantly sick.

We were living in the prison that serious illness creates, a life ruled by doctors and hospitalizations. We were also in such shock on so many levels that as a family, we just pulled our resources together to survive, leaving healing on many other levels alone until there was some time and energy available for it, although we did not recognize that at the time. We just did what we had to do.

I remember feeling that my body had betrayed me, that I never could have believed that life could be so cruel. In addition, Steve's position as a management consultant for a large investment banking firm had been eliminated just two weeks before my first surgery, a casualty in one of many corporate cutbacks that caused untold hardships for so many. We thought it would be only a short imposed "vacation" but that was not the case. It was quite long.

We had expected that Steve would pick up more work almost immediately, as he had never had any down time in more than 20 years in his field. Instead, no offers were forth-coming. He sent out hundreds of resumes and it was as if he had fallen off the edge of the earth. There were very few responses, and no matches. Until this time, head hunters were always calling with new positions for him to consider. Now the phone never rang. The silence was deafening, and so very strange and unexpected for us. At one point Steve joked about how the Lord was not hearing him correctly; he was praying for a job but the Lord had sent him a Job, as in the **Book of Job**.

Steve then developed serious back problems in response to the stress of my illness and the fact that he couldn't find work. He spent several weeks off his feet, flat out on his back in the middle of the family room floor, adding the stress of whether he would need surgery and not be able to return to work for even longer.

To our amazement and gratitude, a short prayer with Steve one evening by the members of our little prayer group brought him immediately back to his feet. The orthopedist was thoroughly surprised when Steve went to see him again; he told Steve that he had fully expected that surgery would be necessary. Again the Lord had come through, but if we had not prayed for him, we can never be sure that he would have been healed as much as he was. He still has a weakness in his back and has to be careful, but the initial agony of a slipped disc was gone in the space of five minutes. We praised the Lord for His goodness and still do.

Each day was a struggle. My mom came up from her home in Florida for a few weeks to help out as much as she could. She was always there when I was seriously sick and I really loved her for it. Life changed drastically without an income coming in, while expenses for three children and everyday living kept coming in. It was an incredible experience, one that taught us a great deal.

We realized that we were literally on the outside looking in to the world we had once been a part of. All it had taken was losing our source of income for an extended period. I remember watching television and noticing just how many ads for new cars, expensive vacations and all sorts of luxuries were being flashed at us. We were watching every penny, so that was all impossible for us. We have never spent very much on luxuries with big price tags simply because trinkets don't bring happiness, and our money is best spent helping others. But it was the knowledge that we were no longer like those around us — people with jobs and security. I experienced being very much alone, despite the help we received in the form of meals from our friends in the parish. It is a humiliating thing to talk about the possibility of losing one's home. It is a very difficult world.

I know now from experience a little bit of what it is to be poor in a rich country, what it has to be like for children growing up in the slums who know that just about everything they see is beyond their reach. It is almost like living in a foreign country. Although I had never put my sense of security in money, I realized on a deeper level how fragile life is. Things can change instantly, and life as one knows it can become a nightmare. But we hung onto the fact that life can change positively just as easily as it can change negatively, and we trusted the Lord to get us through.

I could never again take advertising seriously. This time gave me the opportunity to see the world around me in a much clearer light. The "mantra" on television, in the papers, in magazines is "sell, sell, sell" and "buy, buy, buy" — whether people need things or not. And the lessons of a materialistic culture turned me off forever, as nothing had ever done before, to greed and the need to own too many possessions.

Steve finally did begin to work again towards the end of 1990. In retrospect, he believes that it was far more important for him to be home with me and that is probably why the job market had totally dried up for him. God uses all circumstances for good for those who love Him. It was years before we caught up financially, but some things are more important than money.

As we moved into 1991, I still fought constant nausea and wondered if I would ever feel well again. It certainly didn't seem as if I was going to be all right. I began to wonder whether I had understood the Lord correctly about the meaning of "all right." I have misunderstood Him in the past. But that peace still was deep in my spirit.

In fact, the entire year had been one of a very deep peace, of an increased sense of God's Presence without the energy to experience the "warm fuzzies" of many consolations. Unlike the "Dark Night" of my younger days, I didn't experience that God had left me. Rather, my sense of His nearness was so immediate that it almost frightened me. I knew that He was with me in a place so deep that nothing could move or change it. I think that feelings can act as a kind of cushion that makes it possible for us to bear the Presence of God on this side of eternity.

Because of the extent of my surgery, recurring infections and bad scarring leaving enormous amounts of adhesions, my kidneys had been under great stress over that year. My kidney function now began to drop. Toward the end of 1990, tests indicated that I was well below the 50 percent mark where problems usually start to occur. I felt really sick and as the numbers continued to drop I experienced something new. For the first time since the whole ordeal had begun over a year ago, I felt as if I was losing the battle.

I just didn't have the energy to continue and I had been told that if I should go below 25 percent function, it was almost certain that I would eventually need dialysis and a transplant. It seemed to me at the time that a drop that drastic was considered to be some kind of possibility. The prospect of more surgery in my weakened state just seemed too much to bear. Then I began to experience a change in my perception of time.

If my doctors or family members had tried to tell me that nothing was seriously wrong with me I could not have believed them, because my body clock was telling me otherwise.

The best way I can describe what happened to me was that I felt as if I was standing still in Grand Central Station in New York City at rush hour, and the whole world was dashing by at 90 miles per hour. Time was slipping through my fingers. The days were racing past me in a way I had never experienced before. I knew that I was losing the battle. My kidney function numbers were not that horrendous yet, but something had definitely changed physically and I was losing ground after all.

I didn't share this experience with anyone at the time, including Steve, partly because it was so intense and sudden, and primarily because I never gave up on the Lord's promise that I would be "all right." On a certain level, I couldn't worry and I didn't want to cause any unnecessary concern for my already concerned family and friends.

Although my sense of God's Presence remained steadfast, I began to experience a great deal of inner oppression again. It seemed that the evil one came back to attack me inwardly as he had so many years before during my "dark night." It almost seemed as if I could "see" an evil image of death, could almost "feel" it near me, mocking my belief in God and my battle to stay alive. I felt like it was jeering at me because I was going to die after all.

I believe that I was also experiencing a kind of physical depression because my kidneys were not working too well, so how much of this experience was reality in the strictest sense I can never be sure. I do recall that I ignored any temptations to give up on the Lord, and kept praying as best I could as I had so many years before. I know that Satan is the father of lies and I do believe that he takes advantage of our times of illness and weakness to destroy our faith. It just makes sense that he would.

This period lasted several months, bringing me to early January 1991. One dark cold night that month I felt a very powerful sense of urgency to attend a local diocesan gathering called **Fish on Friday**. That didn't make much sense. It was cold and dark, and I felt quite sick. But I had come to recognize the gentle inner prodding of the Holy Spirit and so I went. I wrote about this experience in an article for a journalism class with my instructor Barbara Fox, so I will include some excerpts here.

> *. . . I can't tell you today what happened during the first part of the meeting. I could only sit and continue to thank God that I'd gotten there in one piece . . . I had expected to see several of my friends from the prayer team. Their ministry is*

healing prayer . . . and I had intended to ask them to pray with me. I was very disappointed to discover that because of the below zero temperatures that night, only two of them, Artie Gurgis and Bob Gellentien, were there. During fellowship time, I passed up a cup of hot tea to flag them down.

The setting was far from "spiritual" . . . We were in the basement of a Catholic school, a typical school "hall" complete with cold marble floors, row upon row of long lunch tables, and terribly uncomfortable metal fold-up chairs. Some of the chairs had been set up in a semi-circle for the lecture portion of our evening and now they were all askew. Perhaps the only thing that was traditionally "spiritual" about the setting was the semi-darkness; only a few of the lights were on, casting long, sleepy shadows. People were buzzing around and catching up with friends, and the din of their voices and laughter filled the entire place. Artie and Bob pulled out a chair in the middle of this scene and began to pray over me in the name of Jesus.

As they prayed with me, I felt as if the demonic image that had been "haunting" me was gradually being pulled away until its presence was simply gone. I experienced a deep peace, but felt pretty much the same physically as when I had arrived. Still, I was amazed at how different I felt inwardly. The Lord had done something, but I didn't yet know what it was.

I awoke the next morning feeling wonderful for the first time in more than a year. My constant nausea was gone. I was amazed. A renal ultrasound the following Monday revealed that my kidney function had jumped up to 50 percent, and my general sense of well being was so improved that I believe that the Lord was confirming that I was going to be "all right."

> . . . *The Lord didn't heal me in a private prayer or even a prayer within my own family, although Steve, the children and I had been praying for over a year. Instead, the Lord called me out to the Christian community, a community open to and empowered with His gifts of healing and discernment and prayer, at the moment He chose. This experience confirmed that there is power in the gathered Body of Christ that can be experienced by praying together as Church, even when it might not make sense.*

That was the beginning of a very, very long healing process. In total it took several years before I could say that I was really feeling better, although chemo and surgeries have left some permanent effects that I struggle with to this day.

I found that stretching my boundaries little by little by adding more activities helped me to get better. By the following winter I was able to ski again and although it took me three days to recover from one day of skiing, I was slowly improving. I also started to work part-time, at first only about two days a week, just to help supplement our income. I finished up my master's thesis at Villanova, graduating in June 1992. It was one of the greatest triumphs of my life, and I thank the Lord for it. And when we finally hit the five-year mark and I was declared cancer free, I felt as if I had successfully climbed Mount Everest. Although it took a great deal of effort and patience on my part, the Lord had once again come through. I *was* all right!

I was all right on many levels. Like many other cancer

survivors, I appreciate each day with renewed enthusiasm. But as a Christian, I know with complete assurance that God alone is what matters in life. I also know with certainty that I will answer to Him alone when I take my last breath; I need impress no one. I appreciate that my family and the love with which I have lived my life are so important when my time to join the Lord comes.

This episode was one of enormous spiritual growth, a time that stilled my soul in ways that have influenced everything afterwards. When one has gone through the valley of the shadow of death and emerges into the light again, there is an inner freedom that only those who have experienced it can know.

But we can all relate in one way or another, even if we have not actually faced death and even if we have done so without faith in God. Suffering and sorrow come into everyone's life and joy very often comes afterwards. Just ask any loving mother if the nausea and discomfort of pregnancy, and the pain of labor, are worth it when that beautiful new baby enters the world.

When the Lord is a conscious part of the journey through tragedy and difficulties, the result of suffering can be much more than an inner freedom on a purely human level. It becomes a work of grace. It is a love letter from the Lord that can be read over and over again, a memory that, although difficult, has been turned to sweetness in the recognition of the wonderful ways that the Lord has worked through the situation.

Our entrance into eternal life has to be like that. After passing through the valley of the shadow of death, we emerge in the pure Light that is God and our hearts can finally rest.

CHAPTER 23

'*Practicing*'
Our Faith

*H*oly *G*round

The little reflection that follows appeared in one of my local neighborhood newspapers in 1996. I wrote it at the request of my pastor, Father Robert G. Lynam, as a representative of my parish. I was grateful for the opportunity because it seemed to close a chapter in my own life and brought me inner healing in areas that were too deep to even verbalize.

Representatives of three area faith communities were given an open forum by the newspaper to express our views on the question, "How do you as an individual maintain faith in the face of evil in the world?" It is amazing how one can take so much experience and growth through suffering and put it in about 500 words. But the Holy Spirit graced me to do it; I am often surprised by the things I write and how God works through them. I include it because it summarizes so much of what this entire book really is about. It is about the priceless gift of Christian faith.

By writing this little reflection, I was also able to take a look back at my battle with cancer with the advantage of several years' distance. It reflects the graces that our ordeal brought not only to our own lives but also to the lives of so many around us. As I have said in so many ways throughout this book, grace — sharing in God's life — is never a solitary thing. Our acceptance of God's Will and our prayers do make a difference in many lives. The article follows:

> *My first response (to evil) is always to find myself "on my knees." When I encounter evil and it demands a response,*

I turn to Jesus wherever I am because He promised to hear my prayer, and I believe Him. He always somehow shows me the next step to take, because the gift of faith is a contagious thing, and always translates into action.

The phrase to "practice one's faith" has a very practical meaning for me. Over the years I've learned to take it literally. So I "practice" my faith like a student practices piano or flute, or like a hockey player spends hours on the ice. Rather than saying, even to myself, what I'm feeling when I encounter any kind of evil, I try to say and pray what I believe. God who is Love somehow will turn this situation inside out on itself and bring good from it, as He did for Jesus. And when I succeed I do it because of a power beyond myself to forgive the situation, the person, the tragedy and very often myself. That's the power of the Holy Spirit, and I love it.

Faith in Jesus is like a candle in the darkness, like a "candle on the water," the lighthouse on a stormy shore in Helen Reddy's song from the movie **Pete's Dragon**. *In the darkest darkness, one candle is incredibly bright. One lighthouse can save a life.*

I know about lives being saved, about Divine providence. I was told that had I not been in Lankenau Hospital in Philadelphia six years ago, most surgeons would most probably have given up on my cancer. But my doctors took the first step by trying to save me. Countless acts of love from our parish community and beyond supported my family through that year of overwhelming darkness while my husband was out of work, serious family problems tumbled in on all sides,

216

and we wondered if I'd make it after all. When my kidneys began to fail more than a year later, the laying on of hands by friends who prayed in Jesus' name had the marvelous effect of turning my health around. The candles around us dispelled our darkness, and in turn increased everybody's faith.

I see this victory of the Resurrection repeated over and over again, mostly in little ways, because let's face it, that's the stuff of life. Then if tragedy strikes, a response in faith has been "practiced." For the best in people, or the worst, comes out in the midst of evil. It ultimately comes down to a choice, not a feeling, and I know from experience how hard it can be to choose the faith-filled decision in the face of great evil when I haven't even tried in the face of smaller ones.

When ordinary people of faith unselfishly give of themselves to help those affected by evil, when we cling to the good with God's grace despite all odds because of our faith, the darkness is dispelled more and more as our individual candles light so many more. The answer to evil is never evil, doubt or despair; Jesus already gave us the answer when He said to love one another as He has loved us. I've come to see that in the face of evil, the answer is more loving candles in the darkness.

CHAPTER 24

Let God Surprise You!

I brought this book to a close in the holy season of Advent. Here in the northeast, the days get short and darkness softly descends very early each day. The chill in the air is both refreshing and invigorating, and the sweet scent of burning hardwood lingers as fireplaces begin to warm homes once again. Christmas lights sparkle in the darkness, and for me they have always signified the light of Christ who dispels all of our inner darkness, like the candles in the darkness mentioned in the last chapter.

It seems fitting that I concluded in Advent. Just remembering all the good things the Lord has done for me has a way of bringing me to a deep inner silence that is very much like the silence and patient waiting of Advent itself. For God has always come to me in inner silence, even in the midst of great activity. God is beautiful in how He reveals Himself through the world He created, yet the Lord has taught me that we cannot really know Him if what we see is where we stop. We must go beneath what we see into that deep inner silence of faith in Jesus as Lord where He alone can speak to our hearts.

It was in silence that Jesus first made Himself known to me from the tabernacle in my parish church. And He constantly brings me back to that inner silence where He speaks without words, always rooted in His Eucharistic Presence at Mass and in His Word.

It was in holy silence that Jesus came to us over 2,000 years ago. There were no announcements heard around the world on real-time cable TV, and toys of the newborn Savior of the world were not available before His birth. It was a very humble entrance for a very great Person. He literally surrendered Himself to us.

God still comes to us in that incredible, humble silence. He has no need to try to impress us. He remains among us as the "smallest" of us all, and that is where I believe that He is the greatest, especially when He daily surrenders Himself to us in Eucharist.

It is in Jesus' self-revelation of God as humility that I find Him to be most beautiful and most lovable. It is a humility that is totally self-giving — from the Father who gives His only Son — to the Son who shed the very last drop of His Precious Blood and gave His very last breath on the Cross for us — to the Holy Spirit, who sanctifies us and makes us God's adopted children.

Ours is a humble God with a sense of humor, deep sensitivity, compassion, kindness and affection — a God who has become like us in all things but sin — who is our friend, our companion in life and our saving, loving Redeemer. His love and mercy continue to set us free every day to come above the pettiness and false gods of human life, and pick us up and forgive us when we fall.

God is mystery (***Catholic Catechism #206***). He is love (***CC #218-221).*** He is the Lord of life (***CC #2258***). He is truth (***Catholic Catechism #215-17***). He is all that we need. In Him I love my husband, children, grandchildren, family, friends and enemies. I am at peace — a steady, abiding peace that only He can give.

I cannot imagine life without Jesus. For He is one with the Father (***John 10:30***), and reveals the Father to us. Through faith in Jesus I am constantly healed and I live to praise Him forever for His goodness. Each day confirms that faith in Jesus can never be irrelevant or trivial — too often the description of Christian faith by an ever more openly hostile anti-Judeo-Christian world. Our lives and our very existence are so fragile. No amount of scientific discoveries could possibly begin to unravel the complexities of the mystery of life, for God is the source of life and to know Him we need eternity, for He is eternal. He is eternal Truth.

We live in a world that says truth is relative, but that is not true. When I experienced Jesus' Presence in my hospital room, it was very clear to me that revealed truth cannot be redefined by any generation, for God is unchangeable. All the doctrine that I was taught as a child by the good Felician Sisters in Brooklyn is true. Jesus says, "I am the Way, the Truth and the Life" (***John 14:6***) and "If you remain in my word, you will truly be my disciples, and you will know the truth, and the truth will set you free" (***John 8:29***). He speaks through the Holy Spirit who guides His Church through the ages from the time of the Apostles. And He says, "Come to Me, and I will give you My love and My life. And I will change *you*." And we must have the heart of a child to be able to accept the freedom He offers.

I thank the Lord profusely for all of the ways that He has made His presence known, for they offer glimpses of our true destiny — to spend eternity with our Father where all tears shall cease and everlasting joy will be ours in union with Him at last. But experiences of God *are not* God in and of themselves. As I said earlier, He is beyond our experiences. He is found in the deep inner silence of faith, and faith is tested on the Cross.

In and of itself suffering is evil and not something that we need to seek out. However, I have learned that there is a beauty in the Cross which surpasses all the joy that earth can offer, and that is a deep mystery of our faith. Suffering uniquely forces us to remain "in the present moment" more than any other human experience. The beauty of suffering is found in deep inner silence, in that "place" where only God can speak to us. It assures us that love is always tested by its willingness to sacrifice for the beloved. I have come to treasure the Cross, although I doubt that I ever will learn to like suffering. The Lord has drawn me closest to Him through suffering, holding before me always the promise of Christian hope that accompanies faith and love, the promise of eternal life in heaven. In faith, I know that all suffering will more than end; it will be transformed into the glory of the Lord.

The key to learning lessons through the Cross has been love. Suffering united with Jesus' own suffering unlocks the power of God not only in our lives but also in the lives of others. Saints and martyrs have confirmed that truth since the first days of the life of the Church, beginning with St. Paul who tells us that he makes up in his own body what was lacking in the suffering of Christ for the sake of the Church (*Col. 1:24*). We are the Church on earth today, and the call to us remains the same.

Yet the life of the follower of Christ is one of divine joy, no matter what happens. We are made to love and be loved, and knowing that God loves us — *really* loves us — gives purpose to life. It gives purpose to everything. I used to wonder why God the Father simply didn't "wave a magic wand" and eliminate all suffering in a quick and easy pardon for our sins. But one day in a very quiet moment of prayer, possibly at Mass, I understood at least partially why Jesus chose to suffer and die for us and then expects us to follow Him.

I understood that He wanted to know us completely, to be one with us in every way possible. He didn't shrink from even this awful death in His love for us. If we had to suffer death, He would taste it too because He loves us. And He would take away its evil sting. He would turn evil and death inside out on themselves. He would take the hardest part upon Himself and change the devil's own weapon to kill us into the gateway to eternal life with Him forever. And then He would ask us to prove our own love for Him by embracing whatever "crosses" He allows into our lives.

In my hospital room at Lankenau I knew how generous are the love and mercy of God. I knew that I had done absolutely nothing to deserve His forgiveness for the sins of my life. I knew that His Love covered everything — every deliberately unkind thought or word, every disobedience, every oversight, every mistake — everything that hurt Him or anyone else. He had forgiven them because He loved me completely. There is something entirely unique about God's Love; He can be angry about sin but continue to love the sinner completely and perfectly. I can easily trust myself to someone this just and gentle. He is on my side. He is on *our* side.

The 20th century has more innocent blood on its hands than any in recorded modern history, and the terrorists of 9/11/01 continued the bloodbath into the 21st century. Still, our world today denies the existence of God who is the ultimate goodness, and of sin, which is the deepest, darkest perversion of the heart. The truth is ridiculed as a lie, and lies are being touted as truth. It is only when we acknowledge our sins that we can be forgiven them. If we cling to them and consider them to be a trophy, we cut ourselves off from the Love of God the Father. Our free will is that powerful and real and terrible in its consequences. God Himself will not force our wills. Every day, we have to give our assent freely to the freedom and holiness of repentance of sin and acceptance of God's salvation. "Holiness is not a bad word," our pastor Father Lynam once preached in a Sunday homily. It is what we are made for. But the world mocks us for it.

Like Father Jean-Pierre De Caussaude in the book **Abandonment to Divine Providence**, through all that the Lord has taught me, what emerges always with greater and greater clarity is that the secret of holiness lies in doing God's Will, in whatever way He calls us to follow Him. It lies in saying "yes" just as Mary did, in always living the grace of her "fiat" as best as we can. What we cannot do, the Lord will cover with His mercy and grace. Every experience of His love in this book testifies to His loving mercy, for it is only with God's grace that we can do anything good. And to every grace, we can respond either "yes" or "no".

And grace received must be shared. To be a follower of Christ is to be an evangelist. As we stand at the beginning of a new millennium, as we walk in solidarity with our Pope and prophet John Paul II, we are the privileged generations who will help to bring about the "new evangelization" of which the Holy Father speaks.

That effort must be grounded in prayer. The Lord has taught me that to be about the Kingdom of God is to live and eat and sleep and breathe the **Our Father**, to grow into a desire for God's Kingdom to come in its fullness with every fiber of our being. My lesson did not end when Jesus taught me how to pray the **Our Father** when I was a teenager. Daily I grow into the **Our Father**. Daily I learn what it means, especially in its community aspect. And we are all called to do that.

We need to be "in communion with" our Lord Jesus and with each other. Our prayers support one another; our love sustains us, in community. Our joy is meant to grow in being shared.

I was aware of how much I need my brothers and sisters in the Lord Jesus one day at Sunday Mass in my parish during my fight with cancer and its complications.

I was very sick, thin and weak when this happened, but when I could get to Mass I did. Although I was receiving the

Lord in Eucharist daily at home, I missed being with my parish family.

At this one particular Mass, I was surprised by a strong insight into how I was being strengthened by the prayer of every single person in that congregation. Most of the people there didn't even know me and I didn't know all of them, but I am confident that their prayers were sustaining me.

Some people were very distracted. Babies were crying. And some teens' faces evidenced scowls that seemed to say that they would rather be at the mall instead of at Mass. Yet God works wonders all the time with the simplest prayers. Every prayer is essential. That is undoubtedly why the devil spends so much time trying to keep us from it.

Yet we are not commanded just to pray for one another within the Church. Jesus commands us to share His Gospel with those do not yet know His joy. The power to do that comes from surrender to the Holy Spirit, to all of His gifts, graces and charisms.

Our Bishop Emeritus Edward T. Hughes spoke to a group of Catholic school principals several years ago and emphasized how the new evangelization of Pope John Paul II will come about. It will happen, he said, exactly how Jesus came into our world the first time — through the power of the Holy Spirit who overshadowed a young virgin named Mary. The Spirit of the Lord must overshadow us if we are to become like Mary, if we are to "bring Him to birth" in our world anew, he said.

Most certainly, Mary was "full of grace," accepting all God had to give her, and although we can never emulate her surrender perfectly, we can try. My own experience of surrendering to the Holy Spirit first at Confirmation and later as an adult released the charisms and broke my silence in proclaiming that Jesus is Lord. Before I surrendered to all the gifts of the Holy Spirit, I believed in, trusted and loved the Lord with all my heart but it was as if my tongue was tied. I couldn't speak about that love.

I have come to see through a lifetime of being "schooled" in the spiritual life and spiritual gifts within the Church, that a Church without the recognition and acceptance of all of the Spirit's gifts is a weakened Church. God continually offers all of the gifts of the Holy Spirit to every Christian, and deepens that new life in the Sacraments of Reconciliation and Eucharist for Catholic Christians. But these gifts and charisms are useless unless they are grounded in deep and solid faith, hope and charity. The grace of Pentecost never left us, and is always ours if we do our best to surrender to it as Mary did.

Our Blessed Mother has visited her children on earth many times in the past century in apparitions accepted by the Church, so much so that it has been named by some as "the age of Mary." Her call is always the same — repent and come back to Jesus. Make reparation for the sins of the world. Pray for its conversion. She has come to plead with us to be aware of how much mercy her divine Son is ready and able to shower upon us. She is begging us to respond to this great time of visitation of grace that God is offering us today. She is a model for us; her "yes" to the Holy Spirit helped bring God's grace of salvation upon our world. And in the Lucan narrative, it was she around whom the Apostles gathered in the Upper Room when the power of the Holy Spirit fell upon the infant Church and set it on fire with divine love. Her intercession can help us to accept the gifts of the Holy Spirit and then we have the power to spread the Gospel. We will no longer be spiritually "tongue-tied," as I was, and those already much stronger in their ability to proclaim their faith than I was, will be gifted in even greater ways to change lives.

A lifetime of trying to grow in the Lord has also affirmed the importance of study of our faith. How would I ever have known Who it was who touched my heart from the tabernacle unless someone had told me about the Sacrament of the Eucharist and Jesus' Real Presence? How can we evangelize without knowing and sharing the Word of God? And without us to bring the Good News for the Lord, who will do it?

It follows, therefore, that if it is God's work that we are to accomplish, we have to allow God to have first place in our lives. It just makes sense. For us to do that, we must imitate Jesus in His obedience to the Father and recognize that to love the Church as Jesus does, we too must be obedient to the Holy Spirit who continues to speak through the Church. We also can't pick and choose what spiritual gifts we'll accept from Him and which gifts we'll reject. I am certain God works through the labyrinth of human weaknesses, and writes straight with crooked lines, despite the ways that our sinful tendencies tend to gum up the works within the Church at times, and even cause great and terrible scandals. Thank God that grace far surpasses our ability to thwart its effects and we needn't be discouraged when we experience failure. Failure is an opportunity for increased faith, hope and ultimately, charity. It invites us to change, if we are to continue to sincerely follow the Lord.

I also believe that God will never try us beyond our ability; He will never frighten or hurt us. He is totally trustworthy. We will come by different paths, every one of them unique. But all of our Christian faith journeys meet in the Lord Jesus and in the people who are His Church, with which He identifies Himself when speaking to St. Paul in ***Acts 9:5***.

Together — pope, bishops, priests and faithful — we carry out Our Lord's mandate in this time and place, grounded in His love and teaching. For each of us that means knowing what we believe and always being open to learning about and preserving the faith handed down to us, which we must then hand down to the next generations. The power of the Scriptures is the very power of God, for the Lord speaks to us down through the ages in the Old and the New Testaments.

We share our own joy, our own story, so that others might know how *loved, unique and, by God's choice, necessary* we all are to the Father who created us. We share with them the fullness of truth to hasten the Lord Jesus' second coming, when all will be restored in Him, and everyone will acknowledge Him as Lord. I completely believe that life need not be as hard as it is for so many of us; when we live for Jesus the burden is light. He always carries the heaviest part. His peace is indescribable and more precious than anything the world can offer; His joy can transform sadness into smiles, even this side of eternity, and His love gives us the fullness of life.

There has been a strong Eucharistic thread throughout this book that has woven it together, because in this Sacrament is the fullness of life, the source and summit of our faith. The Lord has spoken to me most powerfully through this Sacrament. As Catholics, we are called to see life through a Eucharistic "lens". God calls us to be a Eucharistic people. And what we have received as a gift is so wonderful that it becomes a joy to offer our faith as a gift to everyone we meet, as the Spirit leads us. Jesus commissions us in *Mt. 28:18* to go out and do just that.

I have come to believe that this invitation extends also to Christians whose denominations' teachings have rejected the reality of Jesus' Eucharistic Presence, inviting them to think again and come back to Him in faith around Jesus' Eucharistic table in union with the bishop of Rome. *The source of forgiveness so necessary for unity is most perfectly present in the Sacrament of the Eucharist.* Although we cannot know exactly what a united Church will look like, I do believe that God is calling us to unity — visible, total, loving unity — in Him, in the power of the Holy Spirit. Unity is fundamental to our existence as the People of God, and bringing about that unity is the work of the Holy Spirit (*Eph. 4:1-6*). We have been divided too long.

Our witness is weak at best and scandalous at worst. We Christians cannot bring about this unity alone, but for God, nothing is impossible (***Lk. 1:37***). This book is a witness to infinite possibilities. God can make us one if we give Him permission and if we persevere in allowing the Holy Spirit to drive out all that divides us.

———————

I am infinitely grateful to the Lord for His beautiful touches in my life, the uplifting ones and the difficult times as well. But I cannot conclude this book without saying that among the people I truly admire are those who are faithful and loving in very trying circumstances, and who do so with very little extraordinary support. I think of parents of a disabled child, or people living with serious illnesses, or missionaries who live in the worst circumstances to share the Gospel, for example. Their visible love is such a powerful confirmation of their holiness and an impressive witness to the world of the power of faith in Our Lord. I look at them and my own faith is strengthened, and I realize in how many ways my own love comes up short.

I hope that in some small way, the Lord has spoken to you through the surprise encounters with the God of Love that I have shared in these pages. They were written to give glory to God Who is alive and well and loves us all with an everlasting and overwhelming Love. They were also written as a prayer, and so I pray that you more profoundly realize each day how very loved you are by our Father. Above all, I pray that you

always come to accept, trust and follow Jesus more deeply in
your life. I pray that you experience the simple, silent joy that
can fill a heart with song even in the most difficult and darkest
of times. For I have come to see that if we trust Our Lord and
try our best to be faithful in the ways which He chooses for us,
no matter how surprising the road we are called to travel, it will
indeed be the best.

    I invite you to join me in a prayer as we surrender together
to our loving Lord.

Beloved Lord Jesus,
wrapped in silence You are
Love's astonishing kindness and infinite welcome.
Multiple eternities could never repay the gift
of loving mercy and salvation
You lavish upon us and upon Your Church.
Thank you for Your Church,
through which You come to us.
Please forgive all of our sins
and never let us deliberately hurt You
or Your people in any way again.
We surrender our lives into Your hands anew
and ask that You fill us
with the power and gifts of Your Holy Spirit.
To You who have opened the gates of Heaven
let our every heartbeat say "thank you",
our every breath draw You in and breathe You out,
our waking and sleeping give You glory —

in mercy and forgiveness accepted, longed for,
desired beyond human longing.
Love that waits
under the appearances of bread and wine
with patience divine,
come to us and in our own poor way,
we will give You rest.
We pray in Your holy name, Lord Jesus,
in the power of the Holy Spirit,
to the glory of God the Father. Amen.

Come, Lord Jesus!

Bibliography

St. Augustine, *Confessions* (Middlesex, England: Penguin Books, 1987, first published 1961).

St. Bonaventure, *The Soul's Journey into God, The Tree of Life, The Life of St. Francis*, E. Cousins, translator (New York: Paulist Press, 1979).

Cassidy, Norma Cronin, editor, *Favorite Prayer and Novenas* (New York, Mahwah, N.J.: Paulist Press, 1972).

Catechism of the Catholic Church (Washington, D.C.: United States Catholic Conference, 1994).

DeCaussade, Father Jean-Pierre, John Beevers, translator, *Abandonment to Divine Providence* (Doubleday & Co., 1990).

Delaney, John J., editor, *A Woman Clothed With the Sun: Eight Great Appearances of Our Lady in Modern Times* (Garden City, N.Y.: Doubleday Image Books., 1961).

Church Documents Reference Suite (Boston: Pauline Software, Pauline Books & Media, 8th Edition):

Pope Leo XIII, *Condition of the Working Classes (Rerum Novarum)* (1891).

Pope John Paul II, *The Redeemer of Man (Redemptor Hominis)* (1979)

_____, *The Mystery and Worship of the Eucharist (Dominicae Cenae)* (1979)

_____, *The Mercy of God, (Dives in Misericordia)* (1980).

_____, *The Role of the Christian Family in the Modern World (Familiaris Consortio)* (1981).

_____, *On the Christian Meaning of Human Suffering (Salvifici Doloris)* (1984).

_____, *The Holy Spirit in the Life of the Church and the World (Dominum et Vivificantem)* (1986).

_____, *Mission of the Redeemer, (Redemptoris Missio)* (1990).

_____, *The Splendor of Truth*, (*Veratitis Splendor*) (1993).

_____, *Letter to Families from Pope John Paul II: 1994, Year of the Family* .

_____, *Tertio Millennio Adveniente: To the Bishops, Clergy, and Lay Faithful On Preparation for the Jubilee of the Year 2000* (1994).

_____, *On the Relationship between Faith and Reason*, (*Fides et Ratio*) (1998).

Pope Paul VI, *On Evangelization in the Modern World* (*Evangelii Nuntiandi*) (1975).

Vatican Council II: The Conciliar and Post Conciliar Documents (1963-65).

Groeschel, Benedict J., C.F.R., *Spiritual Passages: The Psychology of Spiritual Development* (New York: Crossroad Publishing Co., 1983).

_____ *A Priest Forever: The Life of Father Eugene Hamilton* (Huntington, IN: Our Sunday Visitor Publishing, 1998).

St. John of the Cross, *The Collected Works of St. John of the Cross*, Kiernan Kavanaugh, O.C.D. and Otilio Rodriguez, O.C.D., translators, (Washington, D.C.: ICS Publications, 1979).

Julian of Norwich, *Revelations of Divine Love*, Clifton Walters, translator (Middlesex, England: Penguin Books, 1966).

St. Teresa of Avila, *The Collected Works of St. Teresa of Avila*, Volumes I and 2, Kavanaugh, Kiernan ,O.C.D. and Rodriguez, Otilio, O.C.D., translators, (Washington, D.C.: ICS Publications, 1976).

St. Thomas a Kempis,, *The Imitation of Christ*, Harold C. Gardiner, S.J., editor (New York: Doubleday Image Books, 1989).

Lewis, C.S., *The Screwtape Letters*, (New York: Macmillan Publishing Co., Inc., 1961).

Louth, Andrew, *The Origins of the Christian Mystical Tradition: From Plato to Denys* (New York: Oxford University Press, 1985).

Maloney, George, S.J., *Inward Stillness* (Denville, N.J.: Dimenson Books, 1975).

Marmion, D. Columba, Abbot, *Christ the Life of the Soul* (St. Louis: B. Herder Book Co., 1925).

McDonnell, Kilian, editor, *Toward a New Pentecost, For a New Evangelization: Malines Document I*, second edition (Collegeville, Minn.: A Michael Glazier Book, The Liturgical Press, 1993).

McDonnell, Kilian, and Montague, George T., *Christian Initiation and Baptism in the Holy Spirit: Evidence from the First Eight Centuries* (Collegeville, Minn.: A Michael Glazier Book, The Liturgical Press, 1994).

_____, editors, *Fanning the Flame: What Does Baptism in the Holy Spirit Have to Do with Christian Initiation?* (Collegeville, Minn.: A Michael Glazier Book, The Liturgical Press, 1991).

Merton, Thomas, *Contemplation in a World of Action* (Garden City, N.Y.: Doubleday Image Books, 1973).

National Conference of Catholic Bishops, Secretariat for the Liturgy, *Institutio Generalis Missalis Romani (General Instruction on the Roman Missal)*, July 2000.

The New American Bible with Revised New Testament (Washington, D.C.: Confraternity of Christian Doctrine, 1986).

O'Donoghue, Noel, O.D.C., *Mystics For Our Time: Carmelite Meditations for a New Age* (Wilmington, De.: Michael Glazier, 1989).

Pieper, Josef, *In Search of the Sacred: Contributions to an Answer* (San Francisco: Ignatius Press, 1991).

The Society for the Propagation of the Faith, *To the Ends of the Earth: A Pastoral Statement on World Mission by the Catholic Bishops of the United States* (Washington, D.C.: United States Catholic Conference, 1986).

Tanquerey, Adolphe, *The Spiritual Life: A Treatise on Ascetical and Mystical Theology*, Herman Branderis, translator (Tournai, Belgium: Society of St. John the Evangelist, Desclee & Co., 1930).

Underhill, Evelyn, *Mysticism* (New York: E.P. Dutton & Co., Inc., 1961, first printing 1911).

Photos for Holy Ground: A Faith Story

"Sunburst in Winter," cover photo, Canadensis, Pa., 2002.

"Ground Zero," pg. 13; taken from 1 Liberty Plaza, 39th floor, 2002.

"Blessed Sacrament," pg. 16; New Jersey State Charismatic Conference, temporary chapel in Hilton Hotel, East Brunswick, N.J., 2002. *

"Celebrating Jesus," pg. 34; Children's Track, New Jersey Charismatic Conference, Hilton Hotel, E. Brunswick, N.J., March 2000. *

"St. Michael the Archangel Window," pg. 42; chapel, Sisters of the Blessed Sacrament Motherhouse, Bensalem, Pa.

"Holy Spirit Window," pg. 50; Chapel, Villa Pauline, Mendham, N.J.

"Holy Spirit Window," pg. 57; Basilica of St. Peter, Vatican City, Rome, Italy; above Gian Lorenzo Bernini's altar of St. Peter in Glory ("The Chair of St. Peter") Metuchen Diocesan Jubilee Pilgrimage, October 2000. *

"Angel," pg. 72; One of two statues on either side of the tabernacle in St. Augustine of Canterbury Church, Kendall Park, N.J.; **"Brook in Winter,"** pg. 74: Small brook behind 4 Brook Road, former location of *The Catholic Spirit,* Diocese of Metuchen newspaper, after a spring snow storm; **"Coal Stove,"** pg. 76, once heated our home in winter.

"Tulips," pg. 80; Flowers given to my daughter Mary Beth became a beautiful photo subject.

"Monarch Butterfly," pg. 88; Golden Inn, Avalon, N.J. Taken while on assignment at a Metuchen Diocesan annual Priest Convocation *; **"Mexican Butterfly,"** pg. 91; Monterrey, Mexico, on Chipinque mountain, above the city. *

"Grandkids and Yorkies," pg. 96; My granddaughters Brittany, left, holds Yorkshire Terrier Rothie, while her sister Kayla holds puppy Suki in this photo taken at daughter Mary Beth's home, 2002.

"Symbol of Mary Window," pg. 100; Stained glass window, chapel, Villa Pauline, Mendham, N.J.

"Piggy Bank," pg. 106; from Winterthur Museum Shop, Brandywine Valley, Delaware; **"Feeding the Poor,"** pg. 111; Barney Welch, left, founder of the Barn for the Poorest of the Poor, works with Theresa and

Photos (continued)

Kevin Walsh, two of many volunteers at a Monmouth County, N.J., produce company that allows the group to collect and distribute good, leftover food to Mother Teresa's Sisters of Charity in the Bronx, N.Y. and northern New Jersey. *

"Little Flower," pg. 116; Annual Oct. 1 Blessing of the Roses, Carmelite Monastery, Flemington, N.J. *

"Delaware Water Gap," pg. 122; Kittatiny Landing, Delaware Water Gap National Recreation Area, N.J., May, 2003.

"Bun and Bear," pg. 128; My husband Steve named Mabel the bunny and Harold the Bear who sit on our bed. Any resemblance to us is purely accidental.

"Lilies," pg. 136; Easter Sunday decorations.

"Imminent Storm," pg. 142; A strong storm quickly swallows up the summer sky in South Brunswick, N.J.

"Queen and Mother," pg. 160; The statue's hand almost seems to point to Jesus in the tabernacle in St. Augustine of Canterbury Church, Kendall Park, N.J. The statue is placed annually in the sanctuary on the diocesan feast day, the Queenship of Mary, August 22; **"Offering"**, pg. 169; Gifts of bread and wine are ready for Mass during a Metuchen Diocesan pilgrimage in the Basilica of the Shrine of the Immaculate Conception, Washington, D.C. *

"Blessed Sacrament Window," pg. 172; chapel, Villa Pauline, Mendham, N.J.

"Gravestones," pg. 182; Colonial cemetery, Presbyterian Church, historic New Castle, Delaware, 2002.

"Crucifix," pg. 188; Above outdoor altar in cemetery of Sisters of Christian Charity on the grounds of the Motherhouse, Mendham, N.J.

"Broken Fence," pg. 202; Bethany Ridge, West Milford, N.J. This fence has since been repaired.

"Votive Candles," pg. 214, Shrine of Sainte-Anne-de-Beauprè, Quèbec, Canada.

"Path," pg. 218; Steps leading to one of the hermitages at Bethany Ridge, West Milford, N.J.

— Taken on assignment for **The Catholic Spirit, newspaper of the Diocese of Metuchen. Used with permission.*

Order Form:
"Holy Ground: A Faith Story"

**LOAVES
and
FISHES
PRESS**

Telephone/fax orders: Call (732) 297-6577

E:mail orders: loavesandfishespress@comcast.net

Postal orders: **Loaves and Fishes Press
PO Box 268
Kendall Park, NJ 08824**

Name: _____

Company: _____

Address: _____

City: _____State: _____ Zip: _____

Telephone: _____

e:mail address: _____

Sales tax: Please add 6 % for products shipped to New Jersey addresses.

U.S. shipping/handling:

   U.S.P.S.: $5.00 for first book, $2.00 for each additional book.

   Priority Mail (2-3 days): $8.00 for first book, $4.00 for each
                         additional book.
   For bulk orders:
      Call (732) 297-6577 or
      e:mail at loavesandfishespress@comcast.net